Living Through History

THE ABOLITION OF THE SLAVE TRADE

ALLAN LEAS

B.T. Batsford Ltd London

JW.
#T 1162. L42 1989t

CONTENTS

INTRODUCTION	3
THE ABOLITIONISTS:	9
Granville Sharp	9
Thomas Clarkson	13
William Wilberforce	17
Charles James Fox	21
Lady Margaret Nugent	24
PLANTERS AND MASTERS	29
Edward Long	29
Phillip Thicknesse	32
Duke of Clarence	35
THE SLAVES:	40
Olaudah Equiano	40
Jonathan Strong	44
Toussaint L'Ouverture	48
Gabriel Prosser	52
James Somersett	56
DATE LIST	61
BOOKS FOR FURTHER READING	62
ACKNOWLEDGMENTS	62
INDEX	63

© Allan Leas 1989
First published 1989

All rights reserved. No part of this publication
may be reproduced, in any form or by any means,
without permission from the Publisher.

Typeset by Tek-Art Ltd, West Wickham, Kent
Printed in Great Britain by
Anchor Press, Tiptree, Essex
for the publishers
B.T. Batsford Ltd
4 Fitzhardinge Street
London W1H 0AH

ISBN 0 7134 5868 2

Frontispiece
The frontispiece shows an eighteenth-century
slave market (illustration courtesy the Author).

Cover pictures
The colour illustration shows slaves breaking up
the land to retain fertilizer for sugar cane, from *Ten
Views of Antigua* by William Clark, courtesy The
British Library. The effigy of Wilberforce is
reproduced courtesy of The National Portrait
Gallery, and the Slave poster is reproduced
courtesy of John Goldblatt.

INTRODUCTION

This book is not about the history of slavery.
Neither is it a book about the history of blacks
in Great Britain. To cover that subject
accurately one would have to begin the book in
the year AD 210. That was when the first
black Roman soldiers were recorded as having
come to Britain. Blacks were in Britain,
therefore, before the English were.

The history of blacks in Britain from that
period, until 1833, can be fairly described as
the history of British slavery. That
observation should not conceal the fact that
Britain's slaves were not always black. In the
Domesday Book it was written that during the
year 1086, nine per cent of the population
were *servi*, or slaves. That was some 25,000
people.

In the first half of the seventeenth century
the black population in England was quite
small. Slaves were used mostly in the
mansions of noblemen, or in smaller
households of those who could afford it. The
huge trade in slaves that peaked towards the
end of the eighteenth century had not begun.
Up till then, famous English seamen, like
William Hawkins, had traded in a friendly and
fair way with the natives of the Guinea coast.
But it was his more famous son, John
Hawkins, who destroyed the fair trade in ivory
and other useful commodities from Africa, by
making the negroes themselves the actual
article of trade. His motives were embedded in
a new craze which had begun in the 1650s. It
was a fashion which in historical terms seems
on the surface quite insignificant. People
began to drink more tea, coffee and chocolate.
In each of these drinks it became usual to stir
in a spoonful of sugar to cover their natural
bitterness.

The place to grow sugar was the West
Indies. The sudden need for sugar led to a
phenomenal growth in the sugar plantations,
and the proportionate demand for slaves to
work the fields. By the middle of the

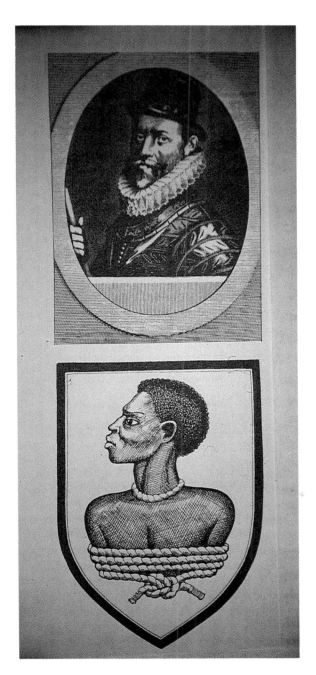

1 Sir John Hawkins and his coat of arms – a slave in bondage.

3

eighteenth century the demand for sugar in Europe can be compared with today's demands for oil. The oil barons and sheiks of today are seen in the same light as the sugar barons were in the eighteenth century. Mass production required cheap labour, and the West Coast of Africa was to provide it. During the sixteenth century about one thousand slaves were imported into the West Indies. One hundred years later, because of the growth of the sugar plantations, 800,000 more had been imported.

This book focuses mainly on those people involved in the British struggle to end slavery. That is not to say that other powerful nations were not equally guilty of using slave labour to generate great wealth. The roles that France, Spain, Portugal and Holland played in the slave trade are certainly as cruel and shameful as Britain's. But none of the other Continental nations mentioned carried on the trade in slaves on quite the scale that Britain did. By the 1790s, one quarter of Liverpool's shipping was employed solely in the slave trade – which in itself accounted for 40 per cent of Europe's trade in slaves. Recent figures tell us that £12 million profit was made by Britain's slave merchants, out of trading over 2½ million Africans. The tragic tale concealed amongst those statistics is that within three years of capture, one in three of those Africans would die. It is no wonder therefore that the powerful movement to abolish the slave trade found fertile soil in the country which practised it on such a scale.

The trade in slaves is often referred to as the *triangular trade*. The explanation is as simple as was the system. Ships left the British slave ports of London, Bristol and Liverpool carrying cargoes of textiles, muskets, beads, tobacco and many other commodities. The destination was the West coast of Africa, where the cargoes were bartered for slaves. This was the first leg of the journey. As these slaves had been kidnapped mostly by African slave traders, it should be recognized that there were people of African birth who must shoulder their fair proportion of blame for their countrymen's plight. The ships, over-loaded with slaves, then sailed to the Leeward Islands, Jamaica, Barbados, Surinam and

2 The Dutch also participated in the slave trade. The drawing is of an African slave the Dutch hung in 1730.

other parts of the West Indies and the Americas. This was the second leg of the triangle, and was called the *Middle Passage*. It was during this notorious journey across the Atlantic that so many slaves died, and were ejected overboard. Those who survived were traded again for sugar, spices, rum and tobacco, which was transported back to Britain, and sold. The return journey to Britain completed the triangle. The ship owners would stock up on British goods once more and the cycle would begin afresh.

Many modern historical views claim that the slave trade was finally abolished more as a result of economic factors than humanitarian

3 A slave caravan on its way to the coast.

actions. The argument today is that the purchase, transport and maintenance of slaves soon became uneconomic. If this theory is entirely true, we would also have to accept that the role played by those in the abolitionist movement is much diminished. If economic factors alone ended slavery, can we give the abolitionists any credit at all? It would not be accurate to hold one or the other theory as full explanations. A purely economic analysis cannot be a fair one. After all, economics is not a force of nature. It is a system totally dependent on man. The critics of the slave trade were often the critics of slave trade economics. Therefore, the two movements which finally destroyed the slave trade, economics and philanthropy, were inter-dependent. There are many present day

parallels that help us to understand why historians are debating who, or what, finally ended slavery in the British Empire. The Apartheid system in South Africa is one useful example, because the problems of racism and economic exploitation also exist there today, as they did during the British slave period. Many politicians these days think they have a firm grasp, and understanding of the South African problem. We can be sure though, that in 200 years time, historians will be arguing about South Africa, as they did about abolition. The debate will be about whether Apartheid ended because the economics of the system no longer made sense. Or because the Anti-Apartheid campaigners finally con-

4 The "Triangular Trade" – the slave trade route.

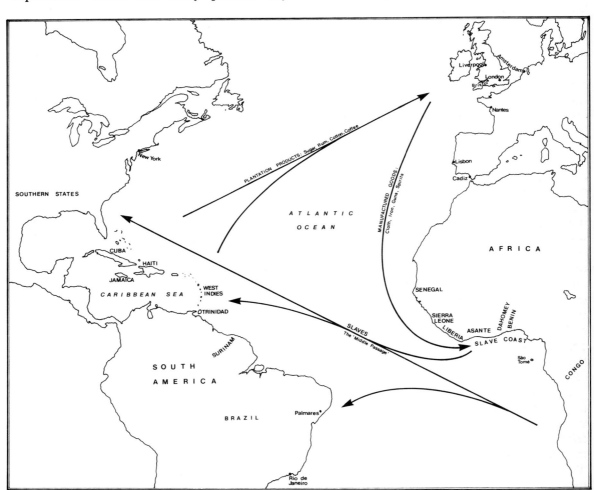

vinced the white regime in South Africa that Apartheid was immoral.

Slavery in Britain and its possessions cannot be seen simply as an ugly piece of history that is best left with historians to argue about. Rather, it should be treated in school and university history books with the same importance as the French Revolution, or the Industrial Revolution. The abolitionists were influenced in a major way by the intellectuals of the French Revolution, and it has been suggested by some writers that the wealth generated by the slave trade actually helped to finance the Industrial Revolution. That view may seem to be an exaggerated one, but it is true that money gained from the West Indian slave trade gave the Industrial Revolution a shot in the arm. Watt's steam engine was financed from West Indian slave capital – so too the South Wales iron and coal industry, the Liverpool and Manchester Railway, and the Great Western Railway. Also, it would embarrass, and perhaps even surprise, the managers of many large British banks and financial institutions to discover that the origins of their companies were financed by slavery.

An honest appraisal of this period of history also uncovers the roots of another aspect of contemporary British life: racism. It is a common myth that the source of present day British racism dates from post-war immigration, particularly in the fifties. That was the period when many black families from the West Indies were encouraged to immigrate to Britain and take up employment in certain jobs where there were shortages. We know, however, that black people have lived in Britain for centuries. And the scourge of racism has been present for an equally long period. We have to look much further back than the fifties to really understand the roots of British racism.

Racism is an instrument. It is a sharp instrument and a dangerous one. During the struggle for abolition it was used with frightening effect to continue the wholesale murder of hundreds of thousands of people. The racists' basic argument was that black people were not human beings at all – but another species. Therefore Christian brotherhood and moral teaching did not apply to black people. It was not believed to be immoral to steal a child from its family, force it to work for no payment, and allow it to die in inhuman conditions. The racist theory justified slavery. It cleared the conscience of all those who profited from the system.

When slavery in England came to a halt there were fears that freed slaves would take the work of white Englishmen and women. Efforts were made to encourage freed slaves to leave England, many actually taking up the offer of a free passage to Sierra Leone. Their services were no longer required. Perhaps it is worth pointing out that during periods of high unemployment in Britain there are those who campaign for similar racist policies. In the eighteenth century it was referred to as *re-settling*. Today it is called repatriation.

This book looks at the lives of some of those people involved in the movement to abolish slavery in Great Britain. The history of British and American slavery cannot fairly be separated. The practice of slavery was similar, and the abolitionists of both countries influenced each other. Therefore there are included in the book the lives of a few Americans. There is also included in the book a short biography of Toussaint L'Ouverture. He was a slave who came to govern the French colony of Saint Domingue (now Haiti). His contribution to the anti-slavery movement was significant and its ramifications widespread. He cost England over £29 million, and Europe 45,000 lives. To quote a biographer of L'Ouverture; "To one man alone this costly disaster was due: Toussaint L'Ouverture. So England thought very respectfully of Toussaint."

The book is in three sections. The first looks at the lives of some of those people involved in the abolitionist movement. The second looks at the lives of a few slaves who suffered under the system. And finally, we look at a few men who fought to preserve the legality of the slave trade. Those men used every and any argument to resist the emancipation of slaves, often claiming Royal assent, as one did in a court case by quoting

Queen Elizabeth, the daughter of Henry the Eighth, who said in 1590 about black people that:

Those kinde of people should be deported forthwith.

She felt that they were taking the food out of her subjects' mouths, and that there were enough people in England without 'blackmoores'.

The population at the time was about three million.

THE ABOLITIONISTS

Granville Sharp (1735-1813)

Many historians refer to Granville Sharp as an eccentric, a man at odds with his image as a dedicated reformer. The intense and often obsessive commitment he gave to a movement which included many reformers and revolutionaries, appears to contradict all that we know of his background. Although he *was* a rebel of sorts, he was also a deeply religious man. That is not surprising seeing that he was the son of an Archdeacon and the grandson of an Archbishop. His brothers were wealthy philanthropists who loved their younger brother and supported him in his views. What they couldn't really understand is why their brother, who was to become a leader of the Abolitionist movement, was content to work initially as a linen-draper's apprentice, then as a petty clerk in the civil service. The historian David Brion Davis wrote about Sharp that:

The role of eccentric allowed him to expose the moral compromises of his society without being branded as a rebel.

That appears to be an unfair, and patronizing view. It seems to argue that he escaped being labelled a revolutionary only because people decided to see him as a social misfit. But by any standards he *was* out of step with both his religious leaders and his political friends. Both groups must have been very unsure about what his exact views were, and where in society he really belonged. Whilst his love for the church, and traditional Christian values, was total, at the same time his political views were revolutionary.

Every morning when he rose from bed, he began the day by reading the Bible or by chanting Hebrew Psalms to the accompaniment of the "traverse harp", which he had invented. He campaigned against indecency in the theatre, and tried to convert Jews to Christianity. These actions all seem to paint a picture of a deeply religious, perhaps even conservative man. But, unlike many other evangelical Christians, he was a genuine political radical.

On almost every central political problem of the day he held views contrary to those of the establishment. He supported seamen in their fight against pressgangs. He supported the American colonists against the British government. He backed the call for annual parliaments in England, and argued against the low wages paid to English labourers. And most important of course, he dedicated his efforts to expose Britain's support of the slave trade.

One morning in 1765 he met a young black teenager, Jonathan Strong. (For Jonathan Strong's life story, see pages 44-48.) This chance meeting, and the events that followed, soon proved to mark the beginning of his anti-slavery campaign. Granville Sharp helped a number of slaves to win their freedom. He offered two powerful reasons to dedicate himself to the freeing of individual slaves like Strong. The first was an almost instinctive and impulsive rejection of man's inhumanity to man. And the other was that he wanted to establish a ruling in the law courts which stated that the ownership and trading of slaves in England was illegal.

Another of the slaves whom Granville Sharp helped was Thomas Lewis. Lewis was in fact an ex-slave. One night in 1770 Lewis was kidnapped by three men, one of them being

5   Granville Sharp.

his former master, Robert Stapylton. He was dragged screaming aboard a ship bound for Jamaica, and was chained to the mainmast. Luckily for him, his screams had been heard by some servants who knew him. Granville Sharp's work in freeing kidnapped slaves was well known, and the news of Lewis's capture reached him the following morning. He acted speedily by getting a warrant to stop Stapylton sailing to Jamaica with Lewis on board. The ship had been cleared to sail by the time the warrant got to Gravesend. So it seemed as if nothing could stop Lewis's worst nightmares from coming true. The captain weighed anchor and sailed for the Downs. All seemed lost. Sharp refused to bow to the inevitable and went directly to the Lord Mayor, and

three judges, to get a writ forbidding Stapylton to remove Lewis from English waters. Fortunately the ship had been held up by unfavourable winds. The officer who was sent to deliver the writ managed to reach it just in time. A few hours later and Lewis would have never been seen again. As the officer climbed on board to deliver the writ to the captain, he saw Lewis chained to the main-mast, with a stick in his mouth so that he could no longer cry out. There were tears pouring down his face.

Granville Sharp could now get to work in his usual way. He took the case to court, paying for it himself. Eventually it was decided that Lewis was a free man, and that the kidnap was illegal. The first battle had been won. The second was to get the judge to declare in court that not only was Lewis free, but that *all* slaves in England were also free.

6 The last commander of a British slave ship.

Sharp believed that this was in fact a correct interpretation of the law. And that it only required a judge to point that fact out and use it as the basis for future judgements – in official terms, to create a legal precedent. Unluckily, the judge in the Lewis case, Lord Mansfield was also a slave owner, and he feared the consequences of such a ruling. So he side-stepped the judgement that Granville Sharp was so determined to establish. Lord Mansfield rejected Sharp's request to make a ruling in court about the illegality of slavery in England by saying:

Perhaps it is much better that it should never be discussed or settled. I don't know what the consequences may be, if the masters were to lose their property by accidentally bringing their slaves to England. I hope it will never be finally discussed, for I would have all the masters think them free, and all the negroes think they were not . . . .

Granville Sharp couldn't push Lord

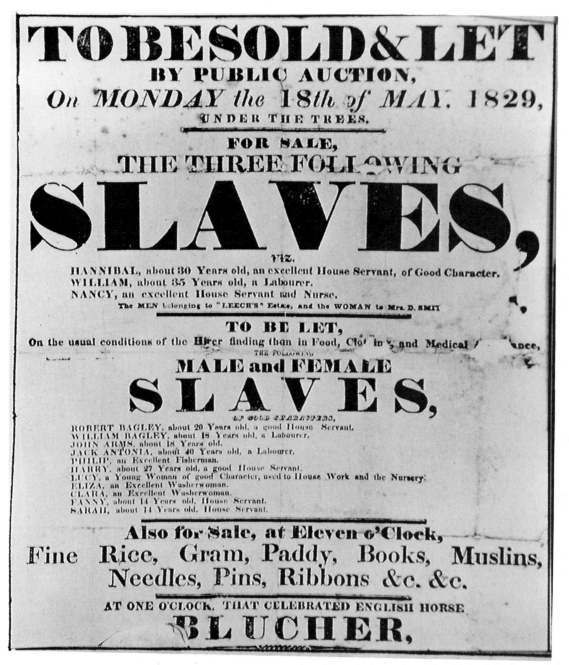

TO BE SOLD & LET

BY PUBLIC AUCTION,

On MONDAY the 18th of MAY, 1829,

UNDER THE TREES.

FOR SALE,

THE THREE FOLLOWING

SLAVES,

VIZ.

HANNIBAL, about 30 Years old, an excellent House Servant, of Good Character.
WILLIAM, about 35 Years old, a Labourer.
NANCY, an excellent House Servant and Nurse.

The MEN belonging to "LEECH'S" Estate, and the WOMAN to Mrs. D. SMIT

TO BE LET,

On the usual conditions of the Hirer finding them in Food, Clothing, and Medical Attendance,

THE FOLLOWING

MALE and FEMALE

SLAVES,

OF GOOD CHARACTERS.

ROBERT BAGLEY, about 20 Years old, a good House Servant.
WILLIAM BAGLEY, about 18 Years old, a Labourer.
JOHN ARMS, about 18 Years old.
JACK ANTONIA, about 40 Years old, a Labourer.
PHILIP, an Excellent Fisherman.
HARRY, about 27 Years old, a good House Servant.
LUCY, a Young Woman of good Character, used to House Work and the Nursery.
ELIZA, an Excellent Washerwoman.
CLARA, an Excellent Washerwoman.
FANNY, about 14 Years old, House Servant.
SARAH, about 14 Years old, House Servant.

Also for Sale, at Eleven o'Clock,

Fine Rice, Gram, Paddy, Books, Muslins, Needles, Pins, Ribbons &c. &c.

AT ONE O'CLOCK, THAT CELEBRATED ENGLISH HORSE

BLUCHER,

7 A typical slave poster. The inhuman attitude to slaves is illustrated by the inclusion of horses during the same auction.

Mansfield to make this historic judgement during the Lewis case. A few months later another opportunity arose when James Somersett, another kidnapped ex-slave, was also forced aboard an English ship bound for Jamaica. The case of James Somersett is also included in this book (pages 56-60), and the result was to establish Sharp's reputation as not only a leader of the Abolitionist movement, but as a man who took on the entire legal establishment at their own game, and won.

Thomas Clarkson (1760-1846)

One could be forgiven for thinking that the anti-slavery movement in England was led by a group of eccentrics, Granville Sharp clearly fell within that definition. And the man who took up the torch after him, lighting the way for the abolitionists, was described by his contemporaries as a nonconformist and extremist – easily equalling Sharp's unique brand of individualism.

Thomas Clarkson has been represented as "plump of face with slightly protuberant eyes. The suspicion of a double chin and a mop of reddish hair. He was school-masterish, very emotional and highly strung." His voice, people complained, "always sounded excitable".

It was also believed that as a person, in the company of others, he could be quite tedious. This opinion sprung from his obsessive singleness of purpose. Sarah Fox wrote at the time that:

I thought he seemed oppressed with the weight of the good work.

Yet despite his physical appearance, and the often negative impressions people had of his personality, he proved to be a powerful mover for the abolition of slavery. His intense commitment to abolition was almost unrivalled. Clarkson's initiation into the anti-slavery movement certainly was unusual. When he was 25 he heard about a Latin essay

8   Thomas Clarkson.

competition at Cambridge University. There was a prize attached to the competition, so Clarkson decided he would give it a go. The question was: *Is it right to make men slaves against their wills?*

Clarkson didn't know much about the subject, so he spent a few weeks reading up on slavery before composing his entry. To his joy, and surprise, he was awarded the first prize. Furthermore he was asked to read it out aloud before the University Senate.

After the reading he set out to return to London. During this journey, he tells us, he began to brood over the subject of his essay. He wrote:

The thought came into my mind that, if the subject contents of the essay were true, it was time for some person to see these calamities to their end.

It was a simple but devastating thought. The clarity of his future actions seemed unmistakable. He described it in spiritual terms claiming:

9 The Anti-Slavery Society. British and American abolitionists meet at a convention in London.

a direct revelation from God ordering me to devote my life to abolishing the trade.

So shocked was he by his thoughts about slavery, that he decided to halt his journey to contemplate his revelation. He always remembered the exact spot where he came to his conclusion. It was near Wade's Mill in Hertfordshire where he dismounted and:

sat down disconsolate on the turf by the roadside.

There and then he made up his mind, deciding on how he would go about abolishing slavery. He contacted Granville Sharp to discuss the issue. The two men were determined that his prize winning essay should be published and distributed as widely as possible. Soon after that, in May of 1787, Clarkson and Sharp met with ten others to form an abolitionist committee. Clarkson was given the special task of collecting as much damning evidence about the slave trade as possible. Josiah Wedgwood, the potter, joined the Society for the Abolition of the Slave Trade, and he designed a special seal with the motto:

Am I not a man and a brother?

Clarkson took up this job, of collecting anti-slavery propaganda, with an almost unbelievable zest. He had decided to travel the entire country, from one slave port to the other, interviewing anyone who could provide him with information about the trade. He began in the London Docks, where he saw his first slave ship. This shocked him and made an everlasting impression:

I found myself for the first time on the deck of a slave vessel. The sight of the rooms below and of the gratings above, and of the barricado across the deck, and the explanations of all these, filled me with melancholy and horror. I soon found afterwards a fire of indignation kindling within me.

He continued his journey to Bristol and then on to the main slave port of Liverpool. During every visit he sought out seamen and ship's doctors who would relate their experiences. These interviews exposed another aspect of the trade that Clarkson hadn't previously understood. This was the horrific conditions of the English sailors aboard these ships. At times the mortality of English seamen was actually higher than that of the slaves. The reasons for this were economic. Slaves were often worth as much as fifty pounds a head, and that was sufficient reason to try and keep them alive. Whereas sailors had no worth as a *commodity*, and could easily be replaced at the next port. Clarkson also began to collect all the instruments of torture which were used by slave captains and traders. He found that these instruments could quite easily be bought in shops. They included iron handcuffs, leg-shackles, thumb screws, instruments for forcing open locked jaws, and branding irons.

It is an extraordinary fact that Clarkson actually met and interviewed 20,000 sailors

during his travels. The slave trade, he now understood, was a crime against English sailors as much as it was against slaves from Africa. He was more determined than ever to stop this criminal waste of human lives. In one emotional outburst he said that:

I was agonized to think that this trade should last another day. I was in a state of agitation from morning to night.

His sole purpose in life was now to expose as quickly as possible, to all of England, the horrors of the slave trade.

Clarkson's anti-slavery propaganda soon had its effects. The slave owners and slave ship captains mounted their own campaign to deter him. He knew that his investigative work was beginning to anger them. This opposition took the form of physical threats and at least one assassination attempt. But Clarkson refused to be intimidated. He collected damning information about many ships' captains. One of them was so afraid that Clarkson might expose him that he organized a group of men to push him off a pier at Liverpool. Fortunately Clarkson was heavily built and six feet tall. As the group came for him he showed aggression which was quite uncharacteristic. It is said that he:

– put his head down and charged like a bull, scattering his opponents.

By now he was also under severe financial pressures. He hadn't been paid a penny for this massive task he had set himself, and to his dying day he remained a poor man. Some people actually predicted that he would come to be known as Saint Thomas Clarkson.

Clarkson was a remarkably effective campaigner. His work as a propagandist was unequalled. And his writing style was described as brilliant and powerful. The author, Jane Austen, did not agree with Clarkson's views about slavery, but she was so impressed with one of his books that she said that she was: "in love with its author".

Ironically, his most forceful piece of propaganda did not prove to be something he

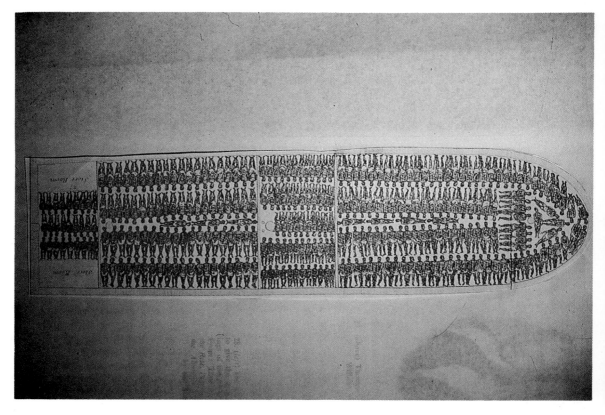

10 *The print.* This illustrated how slaves were packed into the slave ship *The Crookes.*

had actually written, but an illustration. He called it *The Print*. It showed the manner in which slaves were stacked in a slave ship called *The Crookes*. Beneath this horrifying illustration he gave all the information about the conditions aboard. *The Print* showed how 450 were forced to lie like sardines in the ship. During the previous journey, he explained, the ship carried no less than 609 slaves.

It has been written that Clarkson's real claim to fame is that:

When the whole world accepted slavery as a normal institution, Thomas Clarkson initiated the idea of extinguishing it for ever.

Granville Sharp had taken up the cause of many slaves in England, challenging others to support him. Thomas Clarkson took up the sword and dedicated himself to the exposing of the torturous Middle Passage, and the total abolition of slavery. It was now time to find a politician to champion these ideas in Parliament. This role was to be filled by William Wilberforce.

William Wilberforce readily agreed to join Sharp and Clarkson in their struggle. He was somewhat embarrassed however by another cause which Clarkson openly supported. That was the French Revolution. Wilberforce's friends complained about Clarkson's support for the revolution, and warned him to distance himself from Clarkson. Wilberforce recognized the dangers and tried to keep Clarkson quiet on this issue. He warned him about such talk by saying:

It will be ruin to our cause.

Clarkson's views of, and support for, the French Revolution stuck to Wilberforce, despite his attempts to deny them. And both men were henceforth dubbed, *The Jacobins of England*.

William Wilberforce (1759-1833)

Inside the Church of England a small and influential group had formed whose message it was to stress the importance of the relationship between the individual's soul and God. The group were called the Evangelicals. They were an energetic movement who cared more for humanitarian activity than the church as an institution. They were often referred to as 'The Saints'. That title was perhaps too reverent a description and something of an exaggeration, but it would be quite true to identify a leading member of that group as William Wilberforce. One nineteenth-century historian was determined to encourage the crusading, and saintly, interpretation of Wilberforce's fight against slavery. He wrote that the abolition movement:

may probably be regarded as among the three or four perfectly virtuous acts recorded in the history of nations.

William Wilberforce was born in 1759. When he was just 21 he was elected Member of Parliament for Hull. He soon distinguished himself as a politician with both brains and strong moral and religious principles. The abolitionist movement at that time was struggling to find an effective voice in parliament. Without a representative in parliament they were impotent. Another historian of the period described what the movement needed:

an independent man with ability, connections and reputation. He had to be important enough

11 Pitt addressing the House of Commons.

to have the ear and secure the sympathy of the great; he had to have the mind to master a complicated subject and to expose his opponents' lies. And above all, he had to be prepared to devote himself, his time and his money, to the cause.

Wilberforce fitted the bill. His views and sympathies for the abolitionists were well known, and he had the other requirements as well. Namely, wealth, family connections, and a circle of friends which included the statesman Charles James Fox, and more importantly, the Prime Minister himself, William Pitt.

The young MP readily accepted the challenge, and enthusiastically accepted leadership of the movement. During a public speech made in his old age, he reflected on why he was so committed to the cause of the slaves as a young MP.

My grand arraignment of this most detestable and guilty practice, the Slave Trade, is because it is chargeable with holding in bondage, in darkness and in blood, one third of the habitable globe; because it erects a barrier along more than 3000 miles of the shores of that vast continent [Africa], which shuts out light and truth, humanity and kindness.

Wilberforce had always believed that the Conservatives had a stranglehold on the clergy. As the Conservatives were mostly against the anti-slavery cause, the church followed suit. Ironically, Wilberforce, who was religious, found himself being supported by many people and organizations who weren't. This fact was difficult to live with. Here was a religious man, who was supported by people who were referred to as 'godless reformers'. Worse still, he was a man of the establishment, quite reactionary himself on many issues, who found most of his allies amongst anti-establishment movements. The nature of his support left him open to much criticism. A parallel with today's politics would be for a Tory politician to start campaigning for a particular cause only to find that most of the people backing him were

12 An effigy of William Wilberforce. This effigy is currently in his study at Wilberforce House, Hull. The painting behind him, of a slave in chains, was used by Wilberforce to illustrate his anti-slavery lectures.

Communists or extreme left wingers.

Wilberforce refused to bow to accusations in parliament, and in the press, that he was a fellow traveller of revolutionaries. And so he decided to approach the nation directly, by campaigning outside parliament. The historian G.M. Trevelyan wrote that

The hold of Wilberforce and the anti-slavery movement on the solid middle class in town and country was a thing entirely beautiful, English of the best, and something new in the world.

He had performed a near miracle. His arguments found sympathy across class lines, and into the heart of the country. He was appealing to a previously untapped generosity of spirit, re-awakening the conscience of the people. His popularity amongst his electors was almost godlike:

For a whole generation, the anti-slavery champion was returned at every election for the great popular constituency of Yorkshire. He could have sat for it during the rest of his life.

Letters have been found which describe election day in his constituency:

Boats are proceeding up the river (from Hull) heavily laden with voters . . . and hundreds are proceeding on foot.

Another large body, chiefly from the middle class was met on the road by one of the committee. "For what parties, gentlemen, do you come?" "Wilberforce", to a man, was their leaders' reply.

In stature Wilberforce was tiny, and he was referred to as "the shrimp". The writer, James Boswell, decided to attend one of Wilberforce's public meetings. To Boswell he appeared puny in size, and even appeared quite sickly. He described it:

I saw a little fellow on a table speaking – a perfect shrimp.

Then he began to speak. His voice and powers

13 A grotesque dance. Slaves are forced to dance under threat of a whipping, so that their limbs are exercised after spending weeks below deck in cramped conditions.

of eloquence were mesmerizing. One reporter described his speech as:

so distinct and melodious that the most hostile ear hangs on them delighted.

And so Boswell soon changed his mind about the "shrimp". As he listened the:

– little fellow grew and grew. And presently the shrimp swelled into a whale.

Although Wilberforce devoted so much of his time to the anti-slavery movement, he was simultaneously introducing to Great Britain a proud tradition which continues to this present day. By enlisting the support of ordinary people, and organizing them, he had ushered in the era of popular protest. Methods were being developed to establish support groups. The members of these groups paid subscriptions. Public protest meetings were held throughout the country. The entire idea of educating masses of people to express a united opinion on a single issue – and

14 The Wedgwood medallion, which was one of the most popular symbols of abolitionism. It read: "Am I not a man and a brother?".

campaign on it – was a new one. This was the dawn of British extra-parliamentary activity. From then on, countless movements sprung up. Protest and public campaigns became part and parcel of English social life. The State had always been limited in what issues it could take up and solve. Now, what the State couldn't do, voluntary associations and pressure groups could. The movements weren't only political; but religious, cultural and philanthropic. British society was enriched by the methods Wilberforce employed to educate people about slavery and harness their commitments. The heritage he left the British people was the liberating of popular opinion. For Africa, and its people dispersed throughout the British possessions, his legacy was far greater.

Wilberforce was ill when the abolition of slavery bill passed its third reading in the Commons. There was no doubt that it would pass through the Lords – at a price though, as the slave owners were to be financially compensated. He was told the news about the bill late on Friday the 26 July 1833. He seemed a bit better and responded to the news by saying:

Thank God that I have lived to witness a day in which England is willing to give 20 millions sterling for the abolition of slavery.

Tom Macaulay who came to give him the news from the House felt that it had a healing affect. He said:

he excelled in the success which we obtained.

Two days later his condition worsened, and he seemed to know that the end was close. "I am in a very distressed state", he told his friends. At 3 am the following morning he died. Within moments of his death it was agreed that he would be honoured by a burial in Westminster Abbey.

Thomas Buxton, a friend and fellow abolitionist, attended the funeral, and he described it as follows:

I can never forget the scene, as I stood on the

steps . . . the open grave, and the remarkable group around it. The coffin of Wilberforce is placed between those of Pitt and Canning. He had all the distinction man could give, yet it seemed a feeble tribute to one who had obtained something so infinitely beyond. Everyone of any note was there.

G.M. Trevelyan, in his book *English Social History*, pays tribute to the life and success of Wilberforce's final great achievement:

Thus was Wilberforce rewarded for his complete honesty of purpose. He had never shrunk from the pursuit of his great humanitarian object, even when after the French Revolution it had become for a while extremely unpopular in the world of politics and fashion. He had always been ready to work with persons of any party, class or religion who would support his cause. He was an enthusiast who was always wise. He was an agitator who always retained his powerful gift of social charm. He is the classic example of the cross bench politician in our two-party public life. He could not have done what he did if he had desired office. With his talents and position he would probably have been Pitt's successor as Prime Minister if he had preferred party to mankind. His sacrifice of one kind of fame and power, gave him another and a nobler title to remembrance.

In a final tribute, an eighteenth-century historian wrote that the work of William Wilberforce was:

A symbol of great change in the nature of British political life.

15 Wilberforce's *Letter on the Abolition of the Slave Trade*, published in 1807.

A LETTER

ON

THE ABOLITION

OF THE

SLAVE TRADE;

ADDRESSED TO THE

FREEHOLDERS AND OTHER INHABITANTS

OF

YORKSHIRE.

By W. WILBERFORCE, Esq.

" There is neither Greek nor Jew, circumcision nor uncircumcision, Barbarian, Scythian, bond nor free: but CHRIST is all, and in all. Put on therefore bowels of mercies, kindness," &c.—COL. iii. 11, 12.

" GOD hath made of one blood all nations of men, for to dwell on all the face of the earth."—ACTS xvii. 26.

LONDON:

Printed by Luke Hansard & Sons,

FOR T. CADELL AND W. DAVIES, STRAND:

Sold also by

J. HATCHARD, Piccadilly; and W. SANCHO, at the Mews Gate.

1807.

Charles James Fox (1749-1806)

There are very few references to Charles James Fox which fail to point out that he was a lively and irrepressible individualist. Historical dictionaries describe him in a few words as:

fiery . . . irregular . . . lacking balance and reasonableness.

However, the same dictionaries point out other characteristics which explain why he is remembered, and respected by all historians who write about him:

A champion of liberty . . . a man of high ideals and great ability.

16 Charles James Fox. His hat cocked and his hair untidy, this portrait unashamedly represents him at his most casual.

Fox contributed to the movement for abolition enthusiastically. His genuine dedication to idealist politics was only matched by his equally genuine passion for liberalism.

The historian, G.M. Trevelyan, who wrote the book *English Social History*, said that Fox's lifestyle was "free-and-easy". In particular he points out that Fox set the fashion for "dressing carelessly". Today we would call it dressing casually, but a foreign visitor to the House of Commons could hardly believe what he saw. Charles James Fox, and all those he influenced, appeared to have no reverence for parliament at all. The visitor described the scene:

The members have nothing particular in their dress; they even come into the House in their great coats and with boots and spurs. It is not at all uncommon to see a member lying stretched out on one of the benches, while others are debating. Some crack nuts, while others eat oranges.

Fox was held up as the representative of this free and easy society, and he loved it. His passions included gambling, debating, village cricket, poetry, history and "freedom for mankind". It was said of him that his favourtie past-time was:

Spending a long wet day at Holkham sitting under a hedge, regardless of the rain, making friends with a ploughman who explained to him the mystery of turnips.

But what of his contribution to the anti-slavery movement? Could anyone take James Fox seriously? Not only was he taken seriously, but his views were often feared – particularly at the time of the French Revolution. The overthrow of the aristocratic regime in France represented the dawning of a new, and free, age for some politicians – though it terrified others. As the revolution began, Charles Fox commented:

How much the greatest event it is that ever happened in the world, and how much the best!

And as the revolutionary fervour crossed the Channel to England, the abolitionists began to believe that their time had arrived. The great revolutionary cry of "Liberty, Equality and Fraternity" was sweeping Europe, and the abolitionists believed that they were ideals which had to embrace the slave's struggle for freedom. Soon, however, the revolutionaries in France lost their way, and the humanitarian ideals they chanted turned into vengeful blood letting.

Fox and his supporters were caught between two stools. They had joyously welcomed news of the French Revolution, but were later faced with the horrors of its aftermath. Finally, in 1793, France declared war against England.

The days of liberalism were quite suddenly over. The abolitionists were forced to stress that they were not a revolutionary force. After a violent slave revolt in San Domingo they went to every length to portray themselves as a reasonable and law abiding organization. But their arguments were smothered by a propaganda campaign which accused them of anarchy and murder. Moderation became the key word in parliament. "Let us have moderate slavery", it was said. Charles Fox, however, refused to be intimidated by the reactionary tide, and he continued to argue his case. In a passionate and brilliant speech to the House he argued:

How can you carry on the slave trade moderately? How can a country be pillaged and destroyed in moderation? We cannot modify injustice. The question is to what period we shall prolong it. Some think we should be unjust for ten years; others appear to think it is enough to be unjust for ten years. Others that the present century should continue in disgrace, and that justice should commence its operation with the opening of another. My honourable friends, I believe this traffic in slaves to be impolitic; I know it to be inhuman; I am certain it is unjust . . . .

It was a famous debate. William Pitt also contributed to it. His argument was that Great Britain must act on its own to abolish slavery. He said:

We cannot wait for other nations to act with us. Ours is the largest share of the slave trade, and ours is the deepest guilt. We cannot wait until a thousand favourable circumstances unite together.

17 An abolitionist's drawing of emancipation from slavery. Care has been taken to place a bible on the bench beside the woman. The symbols of slavery are being buried.

Charles James Fox had many influential supporters in the House of Commons. He was a great orator and he also had massive public support for his anti-slavery views. Why then did he fail, time and time again, to make any headway in the Houses of Parliament?

One of the reasons was that although the abolitionists in the House of Commons appeared, at times, to be rebels, the fact is that they were very much a part of the establishment. On his deathbed, Charles Fox said:

I have lived happy.

He meant it. G.M. Trevelyan strongly makes the point that Charles Fox and his supporters could hardly be considered *men of the people.*

Perhaps no set of men and women since the world began enjoyed so many different sides of life, with such zest, as the English upper class at this period. The literary, the sporting, the fashionable sets were one and the same. In versatility of action and enjoyment, Fox represented the society in which he was so long the leading figure. The hour was theirs and it was golden.

So we are still left with the following doubts.

Was Fox a genuine revolutionary? Would he really have welcomed an overthrow of the British Parliament? And was he really prepared to give up the luxuries of his position and wealth for his ideals? Terence Brady and Evan Jones, two writers about the abolitionist movement, deal with these questions:

The men bent on reform were at great pains not to insult or condemn this rich and powerful class of people, preferring to attack the system and not the men who ran it. The richer abolitionists rubbed shoulders constantly with their opponents, as they shared mutual interests in most things except slavery.

There lies part of the answer. It was not enough to be an idealist, not enough to be passionate about one's politics. Believing oneself to be a humanitarian did precious little to solve the problems of the oppressed. Charles Fox genuinely believed in the importance of ending slavery. So too did many of his fellow parliamentarians. But they were all, neverthe-less, part of the elite establishment that profited from slavery. And membership of that society was, possibly, just that little bit more important.

Lady Margaret Nugent (1771-1834)

Lady Margaret Nugent fits uncomfortably into this section of the book. She was not a member of any anti-slavery movement, and was not known to campaign publicly for the ending of slavery. It would not be fair therefore to applaud her work alongside those others in this section who did.

Her single contribution to our understanding of the period was her journal. In it she wrote the account of a white woman living in Jamaica. Her story is a valuable one to us, as it is a unique account from a woman's point of view. It is apparent in her journal that it was not written as a propagandist attack on

slavery. Her views on black people, and their treatment on Jamaica, are described in an honest but patronizing way. That is, she makes it clear to the reader her rejection of the horrifying condition of slaves on the island, but similarly, she does not appear to be free of prejudice herself.

Lady Nugent did not plead innocence, or feel free to attack slavery alongside those dedicated campaigners who did, for one very good reason. She was the wife of the British Governor General of Jamaica.

She was born in 1771. It is not certain exactly where she was born, but it probably

18 Lady Margaret Nugent, by John Downman.

was in the New Jersey port of Perth Amboy. Thus, it is assumed, she was the first wife of any governor of a British Colony who was an American.

Lady Nugent and her husband lived on Jamaica from 1801-1806. During that period there were about 300,000 slaves on the island. Her contact with slaves was for the most part with her own domestic servants. Occasionally though she did accompany her husband on visits to plantations and sugar refineries. Her writings were a day-to-day account of all her experiences. The details of her family life, her discussions with her servants, and her reactions to the system of slavery provide us with a penetrating study of the social history of the island, from an extremely unusual point of view.

On 1 August during her first year on Jamaica, she came to a conclusion about the slaves working in her house:

Reflect all night upon slavery –. Assemble them together after breakfast, and talk to them a great deal, promising every kindness and indulgence. We parted excellent friends.

The reader senses that her conscience is troubled.

She made it quite clear that she was only writing her journals "for pleasure", and for her children. It is not surprising therefore that she doesn't make many *political* points. As the wife of the Governor she must have been aware of the island's history with regard to the slave trade. She must also have known about the mind-numbing attempts to "season" slaves. Seasoning happened soon after the slaves were brought to the island. The planters made a deliberate attempt to break the slaves' spirit and resistance by forcing them to adopt a strict discipline. They were taught the rudiments of English and were not allowed to speak their own language. Every attempt was made to cut their links with their African culture. All family bonds were severed. Tribal customs were forbidden. Old religious practices no longer carried any meaning. All that mattered was that they were slaves to their owners, and to the land they were forced to work. The slaves' personalities were in effect nullified. Their minds were put in what was referred to as a "state of limbo". Many of the slaves felt that in that state they were as good as dead. This belief had a devastating effect on the mortality of slaves during the 'seasoning period'. At one stage as many as half of them died during seasoning.

It was the proud boast of many planters that they had fathered children from slave women. Equiano, in his book, relates how on one island a planter pointed to the "mulattoes" working is his fields, and claimed that "they were all the produce of his own loins". Lady Nugent was soon made very aware of this inhuman and criminal practice of treating women slaves as chattel prostitutes. One day she visited a sugar plantation and met the overseer, whom she disliked intensely:

19 A boiling house. After the sugar had crystallized it was packed into the barrels which can be seen in the background, and taken to the ports.

The overseer's "chere amie", and no man is without one, is a tall black woman —. She shewed me her three yellow children, and said, with some ostentation, she should soon have another. The marked attention of the other women, plainly proved her to be the favourite Sultana of this vulgar, ugly, Scotch Sultan, who is about fifty, clumsy, ill made and dirty.

Many times during her journal Lady Nugent informs the reader that she had lengthy political conversations with dinner guests. It is a shame that she felt inhibited to write in any great detail about these conversations in her journal, but the snippets she has included indicate to us some of her political attitudes. One night the subject of Toussaint L'Ouverture, the black revolutionary, came up:

After dinner I had a great deal of conversation with Mr Corbet about General Toussaint Louverture, which was particularly interesting.

He must be a wonderful man, and I really do believe intended for very good purposes.

Soon after that Lady Nugent discovered that a boy of 16 was about to be hung for stealing a watch. She anguished about the young man's desperate situation. The law on Jamaica was that it required the agreement of three magistrates to impose the death sentence. To her, it seemed an unjust system:

This law of the three magistrates appears to me abominable, but I am too little served in such matters to do more than feel for the poor sufferer.

William Wilberforce was also aware of the ease by which people could be condemned to death for little reason. He referred to the English criminal code as "the abominable system of punishments". Perhaps it is no coincidence that both he and Lady Nugent described the penal system as "abominable". Two days after she had written about the 16-year-old who was sentenced to die, she made a short note in her journal. It said:

Study Wilberforce till breakfast time.

It has been said about Lady Nugent that she supported William Wilberforce and the abolitionist movement. If she did she kept those feelings quite private. Her journal also exposes what can only be described as a sometimes blinkered view of slavery. Given her situation it is hardly surprising that she held opinions that expressed half truths. At one time she wrote:

Generally speaking I believe the slaves are extremely well used.

Was that what she really believed? Or was she attempting to appease her husband, who often turned a blind eye to many of the planters' cruel excesses. If, at one time, Lady Nugent felt that slaves were well treated, at another time she felt differently:

The smallest children are employed in the fields, weeding and picking the canes; for which purpose they are taken from their mothers at a very early age. Women with child work in the fields till the last six weeks, and are at work again in a fortnight after their confinement.

Scarcely a month later she is depressed about the general attitudes of the Europeans. The following commentary is a scathing criticism of the white society on Jamaica:

It is indeed melancholy, to see the general disregard of both religion and morality, throughout the whole island. Every one seems solicitous to make money, and no one appears to regard the mode of acquiring it. [Europeans] in the upper ranks become indolent and inactive, regardless of everything but eating, drinking, and indulging themselves, and are almost entirely under the dominion of their mulatto favourites.

What her husband's friends and colleagues must have felt about this attack on them is not recorded. Of the "lower orders", she had similar criticisms, employing in her writing style a degree of sarcasm.

20 Slaves in bed stocks: another form of punishment that slaves in the West Indies were forced to suffer.

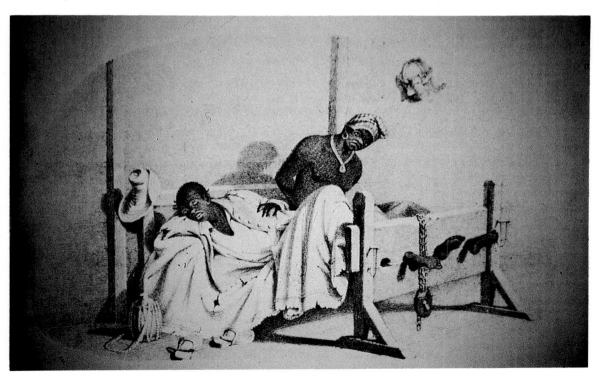

21 Branding a slave.

I have found much difficulty to persuade those great people and superior beings, over-white domestics, that the blacks are human beings, and have souls.

Fearful that her young son would grow up to be cruel and inhuman, as a result of an indulgent upbringing on Jamaica, she wrote:

I am determined to make my little boy so amiable that he shall be loved by all, and not feared. But, in this country, it will be difficult to prevent him from thinking himself a little king at least, and then will come arrogance, I fear, and all the petty vices of little tyrants.

It is clear that Lady Nugent was extremely sensitive to the dehumanizing effects of life on a slave island. Her anxieties about her son provide us with, perhaps, her most deeply felt emotion about the master/slave relationship. There is no denying that she was prepared to abide with the circumstances of her situation. After all, she was the wife of the Governor. To reject the system of government on Jamaica was to reject her husband. She was not being insincere when, at times, she complained of some or other horror, but felt powerless to do anything about it. Women had no power in the eighteenth century – that is why so few appear in history books. The only authority Lady Nugent had was over her home and her children. Her attempts to strike up a friendly working relationship with her house servants, and her determination to bring up her son as a decent human being, tell us that over those things which she had some power, she displayed warm and well-intentioned qualities.

Lady Nugent was not afraid to openly display her feelings. One night at a ball she invited an old negro man to dance with her. Her hosts were so shocked at this behaviour that they couldn't help but take her to the side and warn her that:

Putting them [blacks] at all on a footing with the whites, they might make a serious change in their conduct, and even produce a rebellion in the island.

A few years later she and her family left Jamaica and returned to London. She had two children by then, a boy and a girl. A third child died soon after birth. Not much later she closed her journal, satisfied that the task she had set herself was completed.

Lady Nugent's journal was published, although that was not her intention when she wrote it. On the inside cover of a first edition, held by the British Library, Sir George Nugent proudly wrote a note to a friend to whom he was sending the copy. Clearly he admired his wife's literary talents. One wonders whether he admired her critical and humanist spirit as well.

PLANTERS AND MASTERS

Edward Long (1734-1813)

Edward Long was born in Cornwall in 1734. His father was a plantation owner in Jamaica, where the family had property since the English had arrived in 1655. In 1757, when he was still a young man, he decided to follow in his father's footsteps and establish a Jamaica plantation of his own. His personal achievements proved to be substantial. He married an heiress, was appointed Justice of the Vice-Admiralty Court, and acquired the property in Jamaica that he had set out to obtain.

Edward Long has been described as "the father of English racism". He took every opportunity to express his feelings about black people. They were often based on observations he had made, and his extremely twisted interpretations of them. He wrote about Africans:

I think there are extremely potent reasons for believing that the white and the negro are two distinct species. Instead of hair, black people had a covering of wool, like the bestial fleece. They had no plan or system of morality. They were barbarous to their children. Black men had no taste but for women, and eating and drinking to excess.

If one actually looks at the facts we can easily see how wrong he was. Take for example the Ibo tribe, from whom many of the slaves were kidnapped. They had extremely well organized societies. Not only were they kind to their children but were shocked to discover how brutal Europeans were to theirs. Ibos who were brought to England were unable to understand why English children were often hit, and why so many were abandoned on street corners. And as for alcohol? It was far more of a social problem in Great Britain than it had ever been in Africa.

In the last quarter of the eighteenth century there were already a number of black people living as free men and women in England. Amongst them there were ex-slaves who had escaped from their masters and were hiding with the help of others. They were rapidly forming themselves into a community. In London, where many of them were living, they decided to form clubs and black organizations. Edward Long was extremely suspicious of these clubs, fearful that they might influence those black servants and slaves still in service. About those servants "at risk" (as he saw them) he said:

Upon arriving in London these servants soon grow acquainted with a group of blacks, who having escaped from their respective masters at different times, repose themselves here at ease and indolence, and try to strengthen their party, by seducing as many of these strangers into the association as they can work to their purpose.

Long recognized that there was strength in unity and that these black clubs could quite easily become the recruiting stations for anti-slavery activity. It is not surprising that he was sensitive and alert to these dangers. He had been both a plantation owner and a judge in Jamaica for 12 years. So he was well practised at dealing with slaves both in his fields and in his court. He knew that the only way to contain rebellion was to stamp out any and every form of opposition. Escaped slaves forming themselves in any form of organization must

22 A painting of negro life in the West Indies. This is a plantation owner's view. The two central couples, one black, the other white, seem similarly dressed. The women's faces, except for their differing colours, are strikingly similar, and both own sets of pearls. There is no indication that the fruit is not to be equally shared. The painting is a gross distortion of the truth, but would have usefully served its purpose as a piece of propaganda back in the United Kingdom.

have appeared to him as an extremely dangerous development.

Edward Long was well respected by those who supported slavery, partly because of a book he wrote about Jamaica. He called it *History Of Jamaica*. Because slavery was so intertwined in the island's history he was obliged to write about it. The harsh realities in Jamaica forced him to recognize that the blacks were degraded; but he offered no excuses. Instead, his book set out to justify slavery. He did this by attempting to offer scientific reasons why blacks were both morally and mentally inferior to whites. This argument has been used by racists through the ages and can still be heard today. Many racists haven't felt the need to explain their prejudices. Those who attempt to offer scientific, or factual reasons, often do so to appeal to those whom they feel might respond to so called *rational* arguments. Adolf Hitler attempted to argue along very similar lines about the Jews as part of his plans to seize power and rule Germany. Edward Long's arguments were equally as convenient at the time as they coincided with the British government's plans to rule directly over the people in Bengal. The problem for those continuing to adopt "scientific" methods to justify racism, is that every genuine attempt to measure the intelligence of varying races, indicates that there is no difference at all.

Although it might seem difficult for us

Afba An Excellent field Negroe breeding fast — 90
Sarah Drives Grass Gang lame of 1 arm — 35
Quasheba much afflicted with phthisical Complaint — 25
Rachael Good field Wench — 90
Blanch Ditto and Frank Turner — 70
Sonnet Ditto Ditto — 70
Toney An Excellant Mill Woman — 100
Robyn Moore from Rheumatic Complaint — 60
Cooba Good field Negroe breeds fast — 100
Gracey Ditto at present Sickly — 50
Linah Ditto old — 40
Katty Ditto breeds fast — 100
Katharine Ditto — 90
Priscilla Ditto — 80
Priscilla Ditto — 150
Phoebe Ditto at Times Phthysickal — 75
Salley Ditto has been dropping of late — 60

23 The inventory of slaves on a West Indian sugar plantation. The most expensive slaves are, according to the list, fast breeders. The least expensive all have some physical ailment.

today to understand why Edward Long's views were taken seriously by anyone, the fact is that they were. Coupled with his racist comments was his understanding of the economics of slavery. And in his most important point he was quite correct. The slave trade *was* as important to Britain's economy as he made out. The country had made a fortune out of slavery. Some economists have even argued that the money made from slavery contributed in a large way to paying for the Industrial Revolution. Long's argument that the abolition of slavery would seriously damage Britain's economy was taken seriously by many influential people. More dangerously, many of those people also accepted his arguments about blacks being inferior. The famous writer Oliver Goldsmith, who wrote *She Stoops To Conquer*, was one of those influential people who believed everything that Edward Long had written. In his own book, called *History of the Earth*, he wrote about black people:

This gloomy race of mankind is found to blacken all the southern parts of Africa. In general, the black race was stupid, indolent and mischievous.

The historian, David Brion Davis, reminds us that although few eighteenth-century writers could equal Edward Long's stinging racial prejudice, we must not underestimate how much influence he had:

It is easy to overlook the fact that he assumed the mantle of scientific philosopher and expressed opinions which were . . . apparently acceptable to an influential minority in Europe.

Edward Long's more absurd comments about the intelligence of black people were soon thrown into serious doubt by the appearance

24 A planter or overseer lazily watching slaves working in a sugar mill.

of freed slaves of undoubted political and literary skills. Olaudah Equiano providing one of many examples. Long has left the world with a menacing legacy. These days we call it pseudo-science. It attempts to manipulate a few facts to provide a theory, which pretends to be based on true and comprehensive scientific observations. Pseudo-science is dangerous because it serves to spread untruths, and people who don't know better often believe them.

Phillip Thicknesse (1719-1792)

One day an abolitionist received a letter from a white ex-planter, Phillip Thicknesse. He was reflecting on his years in the West Indies, and he recollected that:

Having lived in Jamaica when too young to think seriously on any subject, you have brought to my mind many circumstances which then struck me with horror. I once saved a beautiful girl from being soundly whipped! She paid me some time afterwards in a manner I ought now to blush at, but when I offered to pay her for her kindness she had shown me, she absolutely refused and said: "No massa my heart beat true for you." But yet surely they ought to be slaves, for do they not prefer a necklace of glass to one of solid gold? Have they not flat noses and thick lips, and did they not fire upon me and wound me with glass

BARBARITIES in the WEST INDIAS

25 A cartoon by an abolitionist. The scene illustrates an actual event which was reported in Parliament in 1791, during which a sick slave, unable to work, was thrown into boiling sugar juice.

bottles from an ambush, only for going to hunt them a little in the Blue Mountains with 50 or 60 soldiers?

Even the most hardened abolitionist must have been shocked to read the account. Although there is a confused naivety evident in the letter, beneath it lies a frightening and sick lucidity. Swollen with pride in preventing a young and beautiful black girl from being tortured, he continues by coyly admitting that he traded this act of mercy by having sex with her. Then he launches into an undistilled racist justification of slavery. Finally, commenting on what he saw as the effrontery of blacks defending themselves with glass bottles as they were hunted like wild animals.

The level of ignorance and inhumanity expressed in the letter is staggering. Perhaps

the abolitionist might have been so impressed by the degree of its degeneracy that he considered giving Phillip Thicknesse the benefit of the doubt. Today we might also give him the "benefit of the doubt" and write him off by commenting sarcastically, "he needs help".

Phillip Thicknesse had spent several years in the English colony of Georgia, before going to Jamaica. His time on the island was spent in sporadic attacks against escaped slaves who had fled to the mountains. The years of warfare with these black rebels bred in him a phobia, and hatred of black people that even Edward Long might have been ashamed of. When a slave escaped from his so called master, Thicknesse considered it a crime. For an escaped slave to resist arrest after having been found – in Thicknesse's mind – only doubled the crime. Hunting escaped slaves was therefore, in his opinion, a perfectly legitimate action – but slave resistance was not. This view was not uncommon, and it serves to illustrate how convinced some of

26 A drawing of a slave revolt in San Domingo. Typically, to add to the impact, many of the slave men in the foreground are attacking white women. The idea of black men attacking or forming any sort of relationship with white women, possessed slave owners and racists.

those people who supported slavery were about the legitimacy of their actions.

Thicknesse has also been described as an eccentric, but that hardly seems strong enough. Some of his views were so misdirected that today we would probably class him as insane. For example, he was as well known for his obsessive hatred of men-midwives as he was for his hatred of black people.

Thicknesse wrote a book about a journey through France and Spain. The second edition was published in 1778, and in this edition he decided to flavour it with a chapter on his favourite subject: black people. It is a classic vitriol of racist dogma which has been echoed through the centuries. About black people he wrote:

They are in every respect, men of lower order, and so made by the Creator of all things . . . . Their face is scarce what we call human, their legs without any inner calf, and their broad, flat foot, and long toes (which they can use as well as we do our fingers) have much the resemblance of the Orang Outang, and other quadrupeds of their own climates. They are in nature cruel, to the highest degree.

Again, the abolitionists must have shook their heads in despair on reading these absurd accusations. Particularly the comment about cruelty – coming from someone who supported and practised it in such an abominable and inhuman way.

At one time, in London, Thicknesse complained publicly about clubs that unemployed ex-slaves had established for themselves.

London abounds with an incredible number of these black men, who have clubs to support those who are out of place, and [in] every country town, nay in almost every village are to be seen a little race of mulattoes, mischievous as monkeys and infinitely more dangerous.

As usual he couldn't resist phrasing his comments about these clubs in deeply offensive and racist dogma; and he was expressing as much anxiety about black integration in British society as he was about blacks organizing their own campaigns of resistance.

Thicknesse's entire diatribe was typical of racist polemic of the period. Quips about intermarriage between the races was a theme that possessed him, as it did all the preachers of racism. Black equality, and black sexual innuendo were subjects that flapped ears in the eighteenth century, as they have continued to sell cheap boorish newspapers throughout the centuries. Unlike Edward Long, Thicknesse did not attract any serious academic or political support. His views were far too virulent, and lacking entirely in originality. They were as much an expression of his own phobia, as they were an exercise in

pure racial hatred. Phillip Thicknesse is not representative of the political view that supported the continuance of slavery – but he did dare to express a malignant opinion which reinforced a perception of black people that dehumanized them in the eyes of plantation torturers, and has continued to find echoes to the present day.

It was written that during the eighteenth century, racism was firmly established as "a principal handmaiden to the slave trade and slavery". The slave trade was abolished in 1807, and slavery in 1833. It was hoping too much to expect racism to disappear, now that its continuance seemed redundant. Racism had proven to be a valuable tool, and a new purpose for it was rising. No longer the handmaiden to slavery, it was to become handmaiden to Empire.

27 One of many runaway slaves in Jamaica who took up arms and attacked the colonial white society which profited from the slave plantations.

Duke of Clarence (1765-1837)

The Duke of Clarence was born in 1765. His father, King George III, had two older sons. He was, therefore, only third in line for the crown. As a young man he served in the Navy, rising to the rank of Rear-Admiral. During that period he formed a sincere and lasting relationship with Nelson.

The Duke of Clarence is included in this book because his political attitude towards slavery reflects quite accurately those of both royalty and the aristocracy. Up until then, those two groups could not lay historical claims to a just and liberal record with regards

to human rights. As far back as 1663 an English company, the Royal Adventurers, was established. This company went into business with the specific purpose of obtaining slaves for the plantations. It was a lucrative company, and many of the stocks were snapped up by city businessmen. A new gold coin was even struck for the company, and from then on English wealth would be measured in it. The coin was made from gold from Guinea, and was soon called the guinea. What had this company to do with royalty and the aristocracy? Amongst the stock owners,

28 Charles II.

served in the navy, where he was stationed in the Caribbean. When he wrote to his friends back in England he assured them that the slaves lived:

– in a condition of humble happiness.

This blinkered view was reinforced by a colleague of his, Admiral Barrington, who said that:

The slaves appeared so happy that he often wished himself in their situation.

Another naive visitor to the Caribbean also wrote back to her family that:

The blacks were the happiest people in the world. But it is odd to see the black cooks chained to the fireplace.

29   The tombstone of a slave buried in Bristol.

were King Charles II, his wife the Queen, the Queen Mother, a prince, three dukes, seven earls, a countess, six lords and 25 knights.

So it seems that royalty did not question the immorality of slavery. Not only did they invest in the slave trade, but they owned their own slaves. King William the Third, who reigned from 1689 to 1702, even had a bust made of his favourite slave. The bust was displayed at Hampton Court complete with:

A carved white marble collar, with a padlock, in every respect a dog's collar.

Amongst the aristocracy it became a fashion to own and display African slaves. The slaves were dressed in smart livery and metal collars. It has been said that in eighteenth-century England there was scarcely a titled woman without one.

During this period the Duke of Clarence

30 The Duke of Clarence – a portrait painted after he became king.

When Admiral Barrington wrote that he wished himself in a slave's situation, one wonders if his wishes also extended to chaining *himself* to a fireplace.

The struggle for abolition, spearheaded by Wilberforce, came up against vigorous opposition by the Duke of Clarence. In a speech to the House of Lords in 1793, the Duke bitterly attacked the abolitionists. He called them:

Either fanatics or hypocrites, and in one of those classes I rank Mr Wilberforce.

It was a vicious attack and he was eventually forced to apologize to Wilberforce. Eleven years later Wilberforce stated that he found:

It truly humiliating to see, in the House of Lords,

31 A carved statue of a negro man servant.

Liverpool. On hearing that the Duke of Clarence had attempted to stop the bill passing through the House of Lords, the city fathers showed their gratitude by presenting him with a gold casket. On it was enscribed:

To His Royal Highness. In grateful sense of his active and able exertions in Parliament.

The message was referring specifically to the Duke's attempts to keep the slave trade alive.

For all his efforts though, the Duke of Clarence failed. His father, the King, was finally embarrassed into giving the bill – abolishing the *trade* in slaves – Royal Assent on 25 March 1807.

Thirteen years later the Duke's father died, and his elder brother succeeded him. He was known as King George the IV. He only lived another ten years, and so in 1830 the Duke of Clarence, the third son, became King William the IV. He became a popular king among his subjects and was described as a "genial and simple" man. Three years after his succession to the throne, another anti-slavery bill was presented before Parliament. The *trade* in slaves had been abolished for nearly 25 years. The abolitionists were now determined to abolish slavery throughout the British

four of the Royal Family come down to vote against the poor, helpless, friendless slaves.

The Duke's father, George the Third, mocked Wilberforce once, asking him:

How go on your black clients, Mr Wilberforce?

In 1805 the House of Commons finally passed one of Wilberforce's bills to abolish slavery. But the House of Lords, crammed with aristocracy, decided to block the bill. To make matters even worse, William Pitt, who supported the bill, died. But the abolitionists in parliament pushed on, and the next time the motion was tabled it passed through both the House of Commons and the Lords – despite another violent attack on it by the Duke of Clarence. The passing of this bill spelt bad news for the slave ports, particularly

32 A punchbowl proclaiming "Success to the African trade" – i.e. the slave trade.

Empire. In effect to free all slaves living in British territory. The vote was passed, and a sum of 20 million pounds was also voted to compensate the slave owners.

The Act received the King's assent on 29 August 1833, and one enthusiastic abolitionist described the moment when slavery was abolished:

As the clock struck twelve, just when the sun was in its meridian splendour, to witness this august act and sanction it by its most vivid and glorious beams.

Soon after the passing of that bill an inappropriate irony took place. The Duke of Clarence had always fought the abolitionists, trying his level best to maintain slavery as a legal institution. However, years later, as the King, it was his signature that signalled the final end of slavery throughout the British Empire – and which brought freedom to millions of people. One writer commenting on this irony, wrote of the King, that he

basked a little uneasily in the undeserved title of the Emancipator.

Four years later, in 1837, he died, and was succeeded by his niece, Queen Victoria.

THE SLAVES

Olaudah Equiano (1745-1797)

In 1745, in a village east of the Niger River, in what is now Eastern Nigeria, Olaudah Equiano was born. When he was ten he and his sister were captured by slave traders and shipped to America. Thirty three years later he could lay claim to many great achievements and exciting adventures. He sailed with Horatio Nelson. He met the Prime Minister of Great Britain. He had 17 editions of his book published. He was appointed "Commissary Of Stores for the freed slaves returning to Sierra Leone", and was widely recognized as the first political leader of British black people. In 1791 Thomas Digges, an abolitionist from Belfast, wrote that Equiano:

was a principal instrument in bringing about the motion for the repeal of the Slave Act.

By far the best version of Equiano's adventures is in his own words: his auto-biography *The Interesting Narrative of the Life of Olaudah Equiano or Gustavus Vassa the African*. Although Equiano was his true name, he often referred to himself as Vassa. Vassa was the name forced on him by one of his English masters, and commander of a merchant ship, the *Industrious Bee*. Equiano wrote:

While I was on board this ship, my captain and master named me Gustavus Vassa . . . and when I refused to answer my new name, which at first I did, it gained me many a cuff; so at length I submitted and was obliged to bear this present name, by which I have been known ever since.

Soon after he arrived in England for the first time, Equiano was surprised to see snow, amongst a number of other experiences and sights which were foreign to him:

It was about the beginning of 1757 when I arrived in England, and I was near 12 years of age at that time. I was very struck by the buildings and pavement of the streets in Falmouth, and indeed any object I saw filled me with new surprise. One morning when I got upon deck I saw it covered all over with snow that fell overnight: as I had never seen anything of the kind before I thought it was salt.

A few years after that his master was appointed first lieutenant of a British naval ship which sailed for the Mediterranean to engage in battle with the French fleet. Equiano was stationed on the middle-deck, where he was given one of the most dangerous jobs on a warship of that period. He wrote about one of the battles:

I was quartered with another boy to bring powder to the aftermost gun, and here I was witness of the dreadful fate of many of my companions who, in the twinkling of an eye, were dashed in pieces and launched into eternity.

Although Equiano was promised by his master that after the war with the French he would be given his freedom in return for his services to the King, he was, nevertheless, sold again. This time it was to another captain bound for the dreaded West Indies, where Equiano had already suffered for a time as a child slave. He was devastated by the unfairness both of the broken promise of freedom and the destiny of the journey. He attempted to organize an escape by paying a sailor one

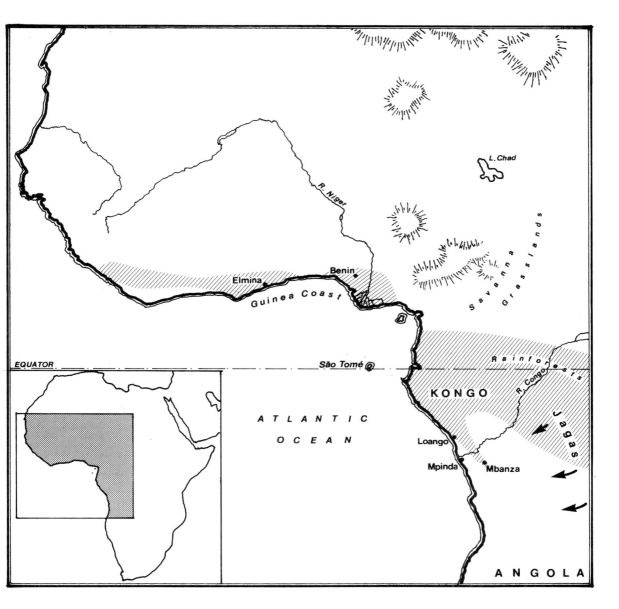

33 The gulf of Guinea.

guinea to provide a boat for him to leave the ship. The boat never appeared. On the day they sailed for the West Indies he lost all faith in men and in any hope for his future:

In the first expressions of my grief I reproached my fate and wished I had never been born. I was ready to curse the tide that bore us, the gale that wafted my prison, and even the ship that conducted us.

On 13 February 1763 they arrived at Montserrat:

At the sight of this land of bondage, a fresh horror ran through all my frame and chilled me to the heart. My former slavery now rose in dreadful review to my mind, and displayed nothing but misery, stripes, and chains; and in the first paroxysm of my grief, I called upon God's thunder and his avenging power to direct the stroke of death to me rather than permit me to become a slave, and be sold from lord to lord.

Ironically, this return to the West Indies did not usher in the beginning of another period of torture in the sugar plantations. Rather, it proved to be the opportunity to win his freedom. Instead of being sold as a slave to labour in the fields, he was sold to Mr Robert King, a Quaker who recognized Equiano's abilities. Robert King decided to encourage Equiano to study, and employed him as a clerk. Equiano rejoiced at this opportunity and soon acquired a number of skills, including arithmetic and writing, seamanship, and gauging★. During this period on Montserrat Equiano was happier than he had been since his kidnap from Africa. But he didn't fail to recognize, and record, the horrors most of his countrymen were suffering:

It was very common in several of the islands, particularly in St Kitt's, for the slaves to be branded with the initial letters of their master's name, and a load of heavy iron hooks hung

★Measuring dimensions, proportions and capacities. An extremely useful skill for those working on ships.

34 A prison scene in Jamaica. Slaves were often forced to act as their own torturers.

about their necks . . . . I have often seen slaves, particularly those who were meagre, in different islands, put into scales and weighed, and then sold from three pence to six pence or nine pence a pound . . . I have seen a negro beaten till some of his bones were broken for even letting a pot boil over.

Equiano spent much of his time on ships belonging to his Quaker master. He soon realized that he could profit from buying certain items easily available on one island, and selling them on another. He was exceptionally successful at this. And Equiano was overjoyed when Robert King informed him one day that if he managed to save £40, he could purchase his manumission. Liberty was at last in sight:

Every day now brought me nearer to my freedom, and I was impatient till we proceeded

35 A slave market.

36 Slaves feeding crushed sugarcane into the furnaces.

to sea, that I might have an opportunity of getting a sum large enough to purchase it.

Soon Equiano had accumulated £47 – a remarkable feat for a slave, considering that a sea captain's monthly wage was on average five pounds. Although his master was shocked, and somewhat disappointed, when Equiano visited him one morning, requesting that his promise of freedom be honoured, he agreed reluctantly to let him go. In response to Equiano's offer of the money, Robert King replied:

I would not have made the promise if I had thought that you would have got the money so soon.

On that day, when Equiano was 21 years old, he purchased his own freedom. After working for a while longer, as a paid sailor, he left the West Indies and sailed for England. In his book he writes of several more adventures at sea, including a trip on a famous expedition to the Arctic. In was during that journey that he sailed on the same ship as Horatio Nelson – who was just a young boy at the time. Equiano also wrote his book, and used it as a platform to expose the brutality of the slave trade. As a committed and active member of the anti-slavery campaign he worked alongside many leaders of that movement. They encouraged him to spend much of his time travelling through Great Britain on speaking tours, arguing for the abolition of slavery.

Equiano's book was published in England and America, and translated into both Dutch

37 Olaudah Equiano, a portrait after Sir Joshua Reynolds.

and German. On 7 April 1792 he married Susan Cullen. They had two daughters, but the first, Anna-Maria, died when she was just four years old. Olaudah Equiano himself died in March, 1797, aged 52. He never lived to see the first Act to abolish the slave trade, which was voted through Parliament ten years later.

Jonathan Strong (1748-1773)

As with most movements or campaigns, it is difficult to be sure exactly when, in history, they began. That is also true of the movement to abolish slavery. Protest against slavery, in

one form or another, must have begun from the day the first human being was forced into bondage. It is possible however, to pin down, more or less, when the first *planned* campaign against slavery began in England. Credit for this has been given to Granville Sharp, who at the time was a 30-year-old junior civil servant in London.

One day Granville Sharp was walking through Mincing Lane towards the house of his brother, William Sharp, who was a surgeon. Standing in a queue outside the surgery, Granville saw a young black man called Jonathan Strong. Strong had been beaten senseless. He could hardly stay on his feet, and was nearly blinded. Granville knew that the man was so ill that he could not wait his turn in the queue. So Granville immediately led him inside. During the treatment, Jonathan Strong explained that his owner, David Lisle, had brought him from Barbados, and had beaten him with a pistol until he was nearly dead. After which he was thrown on to the streets as useless. William Sharp knew that Jonathan would require hospital treatment, and they took him to St Bartholomew's hospital, where he had to spend four months recovering.

The Sharp brothers helped Jonathan to find a job, and he spent the following two years a free man. Then the nightmare he had suffered at the hands of his previous owner suddenly reoccurred. David Lisle, a lawyer from Barbados, saw his ex-slave in the street. Surprised to find him alive and in good health, he decided to hire two professional slave hunters to kidnap him. Once captured, Lisle sold Strong to a West Indian Planter called James Kerr (for £30). Defenceless and imprisoned, there was nothing Strong could do. He was held until the ship that was to transport him to the West Indian sugar plantations arrived. Then, miraculously, the opportunity arose to send a note to Granville Sharp, informing him of his desperate situation.

On receiving the smuggled note, Granville Sharp filed a petition for assault. This was the opportunity Sharp had been waiting for. A

38 Examples of devices used to punish slaves in Jamaica.

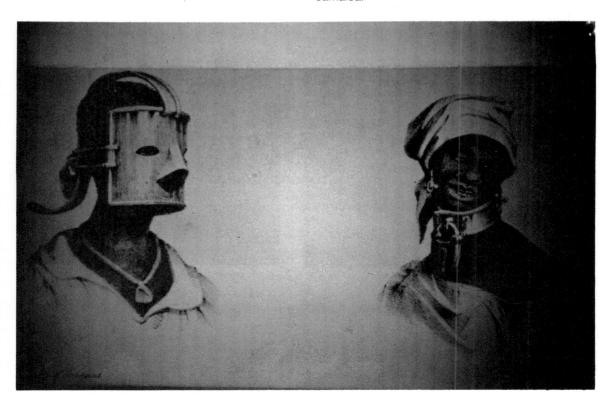

39 A painting by Richard Cobden showing Granville Sharp rescuing Jonathan Strong.

chance to bring before the public the case of a slave whose cruel treatment was clear to all. Sharp had another reason to bring this case to the courts. It offered Sharp the first opportunity to establish a test case in court. The Lord Mayor heard the case and said:

The lad had not stolen anything, and was not guilty of any offence, and was thus at liberty to go away.

The captain of the ship which was supposed to transport Jonathan Strong to the West Indies was dumbfounded. Soon after Jonathan Strong was freed, the captain grabbed him by the arm and reclaimed him as Mister Kerr's property. Granville Sharp immediately jumped in, warning the captain that if he didn't release Jonathan that very moment, he would charge him with assault. Granville Sharp actually wrote about the incident in his diaries:

The Captain thereupon withdrew his hand, and all parties retired from the presence of the Lord Mayor. And Jonathan Strong departed also, in the sight of all, in full liberty, nobody daring afterwards to touch him.

Meanwhile, Kerr was still convinced that his slave was being illegally taken from him. He wasn't prepared to lose his £30 without a fight, so he countered Sharp's writ with

A writ for robbing the original master of his slave.

Public opinion by now had swung in favour of Jonathan Strong. Meanwhile, David Lisle, the original owner of Strong, decided that he had also been unfairly treated by Sharp. He decided not to challenge Sharp in the courts, as Kerr had done, but to challenge him to a duel. The words of the challenge demanded:

Gentlemanlike satisfaction . . . .

Sharp refused, not prepared to chance his life to satisfy Lisle's wounded pride.

The danger hadn't passed for Jonathan Strong though, as there was still Kerr's writ hanging over his head. Sharp spoke to his solicitors, who informed him that in their opinion they would lose the case. They also advised him to pay up and settle any financial demand Kerr made. Sharp couldn't understand it, and no doubt this advice must have sounded like a death knell to Jonathan Strong.

Sharp hadn't opened a law book in his life, so he decided to purchase an entire law library. Then, night after night he studied, desperate to find a legal argument that would ensure Jonathan Strong's freedom. Finally he came to the conclusion that he could win the case, and he published a brilliant article which, he felt, proved his argument. It had

40 A belled slave collar was often used to inhibit persistent runaways from attempting further escapes.

exactly the right effect, scaring off Kerr's solicitors. Kerr reluctantly withdrew his writ and the case was withdrawn.

Although Jonathan Strong was once again a free man, Granville Sharp was somewhat disappointed that the case had been abandoned. He had lost his opportunity to establish a test case which could have laid down the law, and might have prevented similar kidnappings in future.

Jonathan Strong had nevertheless provided Sharp with the motivation to begin his long battle to abolish slavery. The young slave was only 17 when he had been found close to death outside the surgery of William Sharp. The injuries he suffered at Lisle's hand continued to dog him for the next few years, and he never fully recovered from them. He was 20 by the time his court case had petered out, and five years later the wounds inflicted on him led him back to hospital, where he died.

The short life of Jonathan Strong as history records it has not taken account of his own feelings, attitudes and personal remembrances. Instead we piece his life together from legal sources, newspaper records and the few people who knew him. The fact is that Jonathan Strong had as little influence in the often torturous direction his life took, as in the way history recorded it. That is why he is essentially remembered more as someone who appeared in other people's lives – and in one way, in another people's history – as a character in Granville Sharp's struggle, and a bit player in the story of English legal history. We have lost forever the real story of Jonathan Strong. Only he could have given it to us. We must always reflect on that fact, and remind ourselves that the history of someone is sometimes a reflection of how other people judged that person, rather than a genuine portrayal of who he or she really was.

Toussaint L'Ouverture (1743-1803)

Toussaint L'Ouverture has been called many things by many people. He is rarely mentioned in school history books, but those historians who look back on his life favourably, often say that it is he, and not William Wilberforce, who should be credited with the abolition of slavery in the West Indies. Another historian, John Franklin, who was not quite as convinced about L'Ouverture's humanitarianism, said:

During that time [after L'Ouverture had taken control of Saint Domingue] Toussaint L'Ouverture imposed a system of forced labour that was little better than the slavery from which the negroes had just emerged.

Toussaint L'Ouverture was born in 1743 in Saint Domingue. He was the eldest son of an

African prince – and the grandson of an African King. This King, Goau-Guinou, had been captured in a tribal battle and sold to a Portuguese trader. Soon he found himself on board a slave ship bound for the West Indian island of Saint Domingue. Because Toussaint L'Ouverture's family were from royal descent they were given a few privileges which other slaves were denied. For example, their house was larger than most and they had their own vegetable garden. They were also allowed to keep chickens, and tied to a stake was the family's prized possession, a pig. One can understand why these few assets and privileges were so valued if a comparison is made with the lot of the other slaves on the islands. For them, Saint Domingue was described as "the worst hell on Earth". Forty thousand slaves were brought there each year

41 A slave uprising in St Domingue in 1791.

and the death rate was higher on that island than any other in the West Indies. One French aristocrat said about it:

It is a second Sodom which will be consumed by the wrath of God.

The level of violence inflicted on the slave population can hardly be exaggerated. The large slave population was always seen as a threat to the security of the white landowners, and it was believed that only a regime of harsh justice and cruel punishment would prevent an uprising. Historical archives describe many of the methods employed to keep this order. Eyewitnesses have written that:

The most widely used deterrent was the lash. The victim was pegged to the ground by four stakes. He was repeatedly and violently lashed until the skin was torn from his back. The agony was increased by salt or quicklime being rubbed into the wounds or flaming splinters of wood inserted.

A letter written from Messieurs de Larnage in 1744 bore witness that arms and legs were often mutilated as punishment.

Toussaint L'Ouverture was brought up by his parents in a relatively happy home, despite the constant reminders all about him that his fellow slaves were living a tortured existence. He would sit on the mud floor of their hut listening to the stories of his grandfather, the King. They were tales of great battles, and heroism. But most important they instilled in the young boy feelings of pride. Although he was born a slave, and had no other life to compare, he recognized that it was an evil condition forced upon him and his family. Unlike many other people who were oppressed, he never gave in to his oppressors. He did not accept any accusations of inferiority. He wrote about these feelings later on in life:

I was born a slave, but nature gave me a soul of

a free man. Every day I raised up my hands in prayer to God to implore him to come to the aid of my brethren and to shed the light of his mercy upon them.

As a young man he was keen to acquire knowledge. His godfather, Pierre Baptiste, taught him to read and write, and the basics of Latin, French, geometry and drawing. This knowledge attracted the attentions of his master, who first used him as his personal coachman, and eventually put him in charge of all the other blacks on his plantation. Combined with these teachings, his father had passed on to him the secrets of herbal medicine – a skill which brought him much respect. As he grew older he became known for his abilities to cure the sick. C.L.R. James, the West Indian historian, says about L'Ouverture that:

His comparative learning, his success in life, his character and personality gave him an immense prestige among all the negroes who knew him... Knowing his superiority he never had the slightest doubt that his destiny was to become their leader, nor would those with whom he came into contact take long to recognize it.

L'Ouverture knew full well the immense odds stacked against the liberation of the slaves on Saint Domingue. It was the most valuable of the West Indian colonies. Controlled by France, it provided a major income to the French economy. The soil was so fertile that the same number of slaves could cultivate five times more cane than an equivalent number could in Jamaica. France was not, therefore, keen to lose control of the island – not to the British, or the slaves who lived there. These were the political and economic realities, and L'Ouverture decided to bide his time, and his revolutionary visions, until he felt a slave revolt might succeed.

The French Revolution finally offered the key to change. Europe was in turmoil. The famous slogan of the French revolutionaries was *Liberty, Equality and Fraternity*. This call to free all people and create an equal society, frightened the aristocratic regimes of Europe

42 A d'Haitan stamp printed in 1968 which depicts a Monument to the Unknown Slave.

as much as it did the whites on Saint Domingue. Soon the British and others were at war with the French. The white plantation owners were promised continued political and social superiority by the British. Revolutionary France promised the slaves freedom. L'Ouverture knew that his time had come. In August 1793 he rallied his fellow slaves, saying to them:

Brothers and friends, I am Toussaint L'Ouverture. I have undertaken vengeance. I want liberty and equality to reign in San Domingue. I work to bring them into existance. Unite yourselves to us, brothers, and fight with us for the same cause.

The British poured their troops into San Domingue but many were struck down by yellow fever. L'Ouverture's men however

43 Toussaint L'Ouverture.

were acclimatized to the weather, and the various diseases on the island, and won the battle. Toussaint was now Commander-in-Chief of the army, and struck a deal with the British: if they evacuated the island he wouldn't attack Jamaica. By 1798 Toussaint was the effective ruler of the island. His rule was so secure that he likened himself to another man with even higher ambitions than his own: Toussaint called himself, the "Bonaparte of San Domingue".

The final irony in Toussaint's life was that the man he compared himself to finally destroyed him. Napoleon seized France in a coup d'etat in 1801. He was determined to bring Saint Domingue under direct French control once again. With that objective in mind he sent his brother-in-law, Leclerc, to the island. Toussaint was captured and forced aboard a French ship. Toussaint told the French:

In overthrowing me you have cut down in San

Domingue only the trunk of the tree of liberty. It will spring up again by the roots for they are numerous and deep.

He was imprisoned in France high up in the French Alps, where the extreme cold and meagre diet soon resulted in his health failing. He died on 17 April 1803, and his body was thrown into an unmarked grave.

Gabriel Prosser (? -1800)

The history of slavery in America is closely related to that of Great Britain. Likewise, the movements for abolition of slavery in the two countries had similar roots. There had been political movements for abolition in the North Eastern states of America for some time. Religious groups, like the Quakers, were another powerful force campaigning against slavery. Although anti-slavery movements throughout the United States came later than they did in Great Britain, they had their own earlier regional successes. In the more liberal North Eastern States, "freedom from slavery acts" were passed between 1780 and 1786 – in Pennsylvania, Massachusetts, Connecticut, Rhode Island, New York and New Jersey.

Gabriel Prosser was a slave from Virginia. The American War of Independence was still under way (1775-1783). The British commander in the South had already offered freedom to every slave who joined his army. In Virginia alone 30,000 slaves fled from their masters to join the British. The news about the offer spread like wildfire. One slave owner who realized how fast the news of the British offer was being passed on, commented:

Negroes have a wonderful art of communicating intelligence among themselves. It will run several hundred miles in a fortnight

There were so many slaves in South Carolina that the territory was reluctant to enter the War of Independence, fearful of prompting mass slave reinforcement for the British. Even so, 25,000 slaves from South Carolina joined the British forces. And across the South as a whole, one in five slaves were recruited.

The American Congress was in the process of establishing an independent national state. In his original draft of the Declaration of Independence, Thomas Jefferson spoke out against slavery. He criticized King George the Third's attitude to the slave trade, by writing:

He has waged a cruel war against human nature itself, violating its most sacred rights of life and liberty in the persons of a distant people who never offended him.

That criticism seemed to indicate, initially, that a post-war, independent America, would come out against slavery. To the slaves in America that must have seemed like extremely good news. A factor that Jefferson didn't count on however, was the South. Many of the supporters of the war who came from the Southern States were shocked to read the anti-slave clause in the draft declaration. After all, they argued, their livelihood depended on slaves as both investments and labour. So they refused to sign the document. A united front couldn't be presented – either to the British, or to the blacks of America. The Continental Congress, who had presented the draft declaration, finally decided that they would rather lose the clause relating to the freedom of slaves, than those white supporters from the Southern States. Fatefully, the clause that argued for the abolition of slavery was removed. The pro-slavery lobby had won. The dreams held by white Americans were not

44 Cudjo Lewis, last survivor of a slave ship.

to be offered to black Americans.

The Trinidadian writer C.L.R. James describes those dashed hopes as:

Filled with expressed passions of human rights, liberties, dignity, equality, and the pursuit of happiness.

It must have been an extremely confusing time for America's slaves. The British, infamous for their role in the slave trade, were now offering freedom to blacks who enlisted into their army. The Americans, on the other hand, were fighting for an ideal world – but a world which *excluded* blacks. These contradictions were recognized by the rebel forces, and naturally they were extremely wary of recruiting slaves. The danger of slaves in their army, they realized early on, was of open rebellion. And so, General George **Washington issued an order on 6 July 1775 that:**

. . . any stroller, negro or vagabond will not be recruited for service.

The British tactic of offering freedom to the slaves in return for military service, stunned George Washington. The fact that so many slaves were taking up the British offer soon forced him to review his first command. He issued another statement moderating his earlier view, which now said:

All blacks who have already served may now re-enlist.

Gabriel Prosser decided to exploit this situation to the full. But his plan was not to join the British, or the white colonists fighting for independence. Shrewdly, he realized that the colonists' talk of liberty and equality, and the British offers of freedom, must have had a

45 Dealers in slaves. A company who traded slaves in Virginia, the headquarters of the Southern slave business in America.

46 Slaves cutting ripe sugarcane at harvest time. Men and women were both used for this exhausting task.

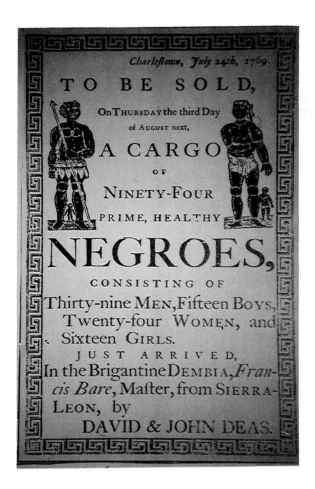

Charlestown, July 24th, 1769.

TO BE SOLD,

On THURSDAY the third Day
of AUGUST next,

A CARGO

OF

NINETY-FOUR

PRIME, HEALTHY

NEGROES,

CONSISTING OF

Thirty-nine MEN, Fifteen BOYS,
Twenty-four WOMEN, and
Sixteen GIRLS.

JUST ARRIVED,

In the Brigantine DEMBIA, *Francis Bare*, Master, from SIERRA-
LEON, by

DAVID & JOHN DEAS.

47 A sale poster for slaves. The sale was held in Charleston on 24 July 1769.

strong impact on America's slaves. And so, instead of joining either of the opposing white armies, Gabriel Prosser decided to organize a third force; in effect, a black rebel army. Rebellion in America was not a new idea, as one writer points out:

There were several hundred slave revolts on record. Rebellion went hand in hand with slavery. Some slaves fought back, ran away, poisoned the owner, even burned buildings. The most dreaded act of dissention was that of open revolt.

The young Gabriel Prosser hatched a plot. On the 30 August 1800 he planned to storm the city of Richmond. It was the capital city of Virginia, the state which was to produce four of the first five American presidents. Throughout the spring of that year the slaves made and collected arms and ammunition. For month after month Gabriel Prosser entered the city on spying missions. His task was to note down all the places where ammunition and arms were stored. His grand plan was to capture Richmond and proclaim the entire state of Virginia as a Negro state.

The night of the rebellion arrived. So too did the heaviest rains for many years. Over a thousand slave rebels had heeded Prosser's call (although there are estimates that Gabriel Prosser had the support of as many as 60,000 slaves). The black army had gathered a few miles from the town. The rain continued in torrents, and the muddy roads soon became impassable. Bridges were swept away and the plantations turned into hazardous swamps. The attack was thus delayed, just long enough for the Richmond authorities to discover the plot and organize their defences. (Two slaves who feared for the lives of their former masters gave the plan away.) News of the rebellion also reached the United States Cavalry. By then the slave army of one thousand were reduced by the storm to just over three hundred. Most believed that a successful rebellion was no longer possible. Finally the cavalry arrived and further splintered the group. Many were arrested, but Gabriel Prosser managed to escape. A large reward was offered for Prosser's capture, and a few weeks later he was caught. Thirty five of the men captured were executed. Under interrogation, Gabriel Prosser refused to give any names of others involved in the plot. On 3 October he was sentenced to death. Meanwhile, news of the attempted rebellion had spread, and slaves assembled for other uprisings in Suffolk County, Petersburg, Edenton and Charleston. Whites across the country were terrified.

During his trial Gabriel Prosser attempted to point out that his struggle was similar to that of the colonists fighting for an independent America. He said:

I have nothing more to offer than what General George Washington would have had to offer, had he been taken by the British officers and put on trial by them. I have adventured my life in endeavouring to obtain the liberty of my countrymen, and I am a willing sacrifice to their cause; and I beg, as a favour, that I may be immediately led to execution. I know that you have pre-determined to shed my blood: why then all this mockery of a trial?

On 7 October he was executed.

James Somersett (? - ?)

There were a number of slaves in England who attempted to win their freedom through the courts. No case was more important, historically, than that of James Somersett. The name of James Somersett is one that has gone down in both the history of the abolition of slavery, and that of English law. Some historians even argue that the result of the case was an important factor in the suppression of the slave trade in 1807.

Somersett was actually a slave from Boston, Massachusetts. He was brought to England by his master, Charles Steward, a Customs Official. After living for a couple of years in England, Somersett escaped. On 26 November 1771 he was recaptured. He was taken to a ship, the *Ann and Mary*, with the instructions to the commander to be safely and securely kept and carried and conveyed in the said vessel to Jamaica.

Somersett's friends, including Granville Sharp, sprung into action. Here was yet another opportunity for a test case to establish a final ruling on slavery. Lord Mansfield was required to issue a writ of *habeas corpus* against the captain of the ship. This meant that it was now illegal for Somersett to be taken from England. Until that was, permission was given in the courts.

On 7 February 1772 the case opened. Five advocates had been hired to defend Somersett. An extremely colourful character, William "Bull" Davy, presented an argument which stated that:

No man at this day is, or can be, a slave in England.

He agreed that if Somersett had escaped in one of the colonies, instead of England, his recapture would be legal. But it was not legal here. He continued:

Have the laws of Virginia any more influence, power or authority in this country than the laws of Japan?

Davy went on to quote an Elizabethan verdict that:

England was too pure an air for slaves to breathe in.

And he added, appealing emotionally to the court:

I hope my Lord the air does not blow worse since. But unless there is a change of air, I hope they will never breathe here; for that is my assertion, – the moment they [slaves] put their foot on English ground, that moment they become free. They are subject to the laws . . . of this country, and so are their masters, thank God!

This argument was novel and quite straightforward. All it said was that a slave was only a slave in the place where he was officially recognized as a slave. However, in England, the act of slavery had never been officially recognized in law. Therefore Somersett's owner had no legal rights over his slave whilst he remained in England. Lord Mansfield found this argument extremely difficult to refute. So he adjourned the case for three months. His hope was that some kind of settlement could be agreed between the parties outside the courts. That way he wouldn't have to make the decision he feared he finally had to. The case continued, however, much to Lord Mansfield's embarrassment. It must be remembered that the Lord was a slave owner himself.

Another young advocate spoke in court for Somersett. His name was Francis Hargrave, and this was to be his first speech in any court. His argument was that there was no law in England which allowed a man to voluntarily enslave himself by contract. Therefore slavery in any form was illegal.

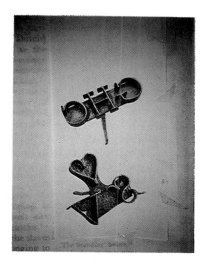

48 Slaves belonging to different owners were sometimes shipped together. The slaves could be identified by branding them before embarkation. These are two examples of various branding irons used.

The last advocate on Somersett's behalf was a man called Alleyne. He wanted to point out the dangers if the decision went against Somersett. His fear was that it would signal the legality of slavery, and that:

The horrid cruelties, scarce credible in recital, perpetrated in America, might, by the allowance of slaves amongst us, be introduced here.

It seemed an odd argument, as slavery was already commonly practised in England. His fear, however, was that the cruelties of plantation slavery might become common practice in England, if the courts removed any doubts about slavery being illegal. All in all, Somersett's case was the most powerful that Granville Sharp had managed to organize. It was soon the turn of Somersett's owner, Charles Steward, to present his arguments. His case was opened by William Wallace, who said that:

It would be unjust to divest him [Steward] of his

rightful property simply because he sailed, in pursuit of his lawful business, from one country to another . . . if the court rejected the slave-owner's right to his property in England, great inconvenience would be caused. There were so many blacks in English ports that many thousands of pounds would be lost by the owners if they were ordered to set them free.

The arguments that Steward's advocates were putting to Lord Mansfield were no match for Somersett's advocates. But Lord Mansfield knew only too well the problems he would create amongst the slave owners if he declared Somersett free. He also knew that about £700,000 could be lost by slave owners in England, if slaves decided to follow Somersett's example and demand their freedom. Simply to be reminded of these problems by Steward's advocates was not enough. He needed to be convinced by legal arguments that Somersett could be forcibly taken off English soil, to be returned back to America into slavery. The key question was whether Lord Mansfield would finally be guided by legal argument, or by self interest.

At long last, on 22 June 1772, the judgement was delivered. Lord Mansfield

49 Lord Mansfield, who was finally forced to rule in favour of James Somersett.

outlined the circumstances of Somersett's recapture and went on:

So high an act of dominion must derive its authority, if any such it has, from the law of the kingdom where executed. A foreigner cannot be imprisoned here on the authority of any law existing in his own country. The power of a master over his servant is different in all countries . . . .

At this stage Somersett and his advocates must have been gasping with excitement. Lord Mansfield had actually seemed to be agreeing with their central argument. He had said that the legal enslaving of a person in a foreign country would not be recognized in England. He continued his speech, detailing the reasons why slavery was not recognized by English law, and he concluded by focusing on the attempt to return Somersett to America by force:

No master was ever allowed here to take a slave by force to be sold abroad because he deserted from his service, or for any other reason

50 Slaves being thrown overboard during the Middle Passage. There were all too many accounts of this happening. The slaves thrown into the sea were either sick and therefore of little value to the owners, or rebellious.

whatever. We cannot say the cause set forth by this return is allowed or approved of by the laws of this kingdom, and therefore the man must be discharged.

No one in the court could quite believe what they had heard. The representatives from the black community bowed to the bench then grabbed each other in joy. As the news filtered outside a massive cheer was heard. The *London Chronicle* reported that:

No sight could be more pleasingly affecting to the mind than the joy which shone at that instance in these poor men's sable countenances.

Once the euphoria died down, the legal profession analysed exactly what Lord Mansfield had decided. Initially, many people had misunderstood the judgement – even today the Mansfield decision is often misunderstood. Lord Mansfield had not in fact decided that slavery was illegal in England. What he had said was that *to force a slave to leave England* was illegal. And until there was specific legislation which covered the status of slaves in England, the conditions would prevail. So, it did not prove to be the final judgement that the abolitionists wanted. However the release of James Somersett led many to believe, erroneously, that all slaves were to be freed – and in fact over 10,000 were actually released. But slavery continued – for many years after the Somersett case, English newspapers accepted advertisements for the sale of slaves.

There is no doubt that the Somersett case marked an important symbolic step in the struggle to abolish slavery. The movement had notched a notable success. The tide was beginning to turn in their favour, and public opinion with it. The anti-slavery movement was gathering strength, and the honour of leading it passed to the philanthropist, Thomas Clarkson.

DATE LIST

210 First black Roman soldiers posted to Britain.

1086 The *Domesday Book* records that nine per cent of the British population were *servi* or slaves.

1513 Slaves introduced into America.

1633 The *guinea* was struck to commemorate the founding of The Royal Adventurers, a company whose objective it was to profit by the trade in slaves.

1650s Tea, coffee and chocolate become popular. The demand in Britain for sugar escalates. The West Indian sugar plantations expand rapidly and the transatlantic slave trade increases massively.

1755 Olaudah Equiano captured by slave-traders.

1772 Lord Mansfield ruled in the James Somersett case that it was illegal to force a slave to leave England. The case represented an important but largely symbolic victory for the abolitionists.

1783 The Quakers present the first substantial anti-slavery petition to Parliament. William Wilberforce was presented with the facts about the slave trade. In the same year the United States became independent of Great Britain.

1787 The Society for the Abolition of the Slave Trade was formed. Of the twelve members on the committee nine were Quakers.

1791 Wilberforce's first bill to abolish slavery was defeated in the Commons by 163 votes to 88.

1792 By now over 500 petitions had been sent to Parliament in support of Wilberforce's abolition bill.

1793 Revolutionary government in power in France. Toussaint L'Ouverture rallies the slaves of San Domingue, finally defeating the British Forces – whom the French had declared war against on 1 February 1793. The British abolitionists, including Wilberforce, are accused of being "The Jacobins of England".

1795 Repressive government measures were enforced which effectively prohibited public meetings; followed a few years later by the outlawing of radical and trade union organizations. For nearly 20 years working class political activity was curtailed. The movement to abolish slavery suffered a long setback.

1805 The House of Commons passed one of Wilberforce's bills to abolish slavery. However the bill was blocked by the House of Lords.

1807 The bill to abolish the *trade* in slaves was passed on 25 March.

1833 On 29 August 1833 King William IV gave royal assent for slavery to be abolished throughout the British Empire.

BOOKS FOR FURTHER READING

General Background
D. Bishton, *Black Heart Man*, Chatto and Windus, 1986.
T. Brady & E. Jones, *The Fight Against Slavery*, BBC Publications, 1975
A. Calder, *Revolutionary Empire*, Jonathan Cape, 1981
B. Davidson, *Black Mother – Africa and the Atlantic Slave Trade*, Pelican, 1961
D.B. Davis, *The Problem of Slavery in Western Culture*, Pelican, 1966
Peter Fryer, *Staying Power*, Pluto, 1984
David Killingray, *The Transatlantic Slave Trade*, Batsford, 1987
O. Ransford, *The Slave Trade*, Readers Union, 1971
F.O. Shyllon, *Black Slaves in Britain*, Oxford University, 1974

G.M. Trevelyan, *English Social History*, Longman, New Edition 1946
J. Watson, *The West Indian Heritage*, John Murray, 1979
E. Williams, *From Columbus to Castro*, The History of the Caribbean 1492-1969, Andre Deutsch, 1970

Biographical
P. Edwards (ed.), *Equiano's Travels*, Heinemann, 1967
P. Edwards & J. Walvin, *Black Personalities in the Era of the Slave Trade*, Macmillan, 1983
W. Parkinson, *This Gilded African – Toussaint L'Ouverture*, Quartet, 1980
J. Pollock, *Wilberforce*, Constable 1977
P. Wright (ed.), *Lady Nugent's Journal*, Kingston, 1966

Acknowledgments
The Author and Publishers would like to thank the following for their kind permission to reproduce illustrations: John Goldblatt for figure 7; Pat Hodgson Library for figure 15; The National Portrait Gallery for figures 11, 12, 37. The remainder of the illustrations were supplied courtesy of the author. The maps on pages 6 and 41 were drawn by Robert Brien.

INDEX

abolitionists 23, 44, 17, 19
abolition of slavery (bills) 20,
35, 38, 39, 56, 61
abolition of slave trade (society)
14, 15, 61
American slavery 7, 52-56
American War Of
Independence 9, 52

Barrington, Admiral 36, 37
black organizations 29, 34
black people in Britain (first) 3
Bonaparte, Napoleon 51
Bristol 4, 15
Buxton, Thomas 20

Charles II, King 36
Clarence, Duke of 35-39
Clarkson, Thomas 13-16, 60
Continental Congress 52
Crookes, The 16
Cullen, Susan 44

Davy, William Bull 56-57
Declaration of Independence
(American) 52
Resistance to; *see* Southern
States
Domesday Book 3, 61

Equianò, Gustavus Vassa
(Olaudah Equiano) 25, 32,
40-44
Evangelicals 17

Fox, Charles James 18, 21-24
French Revolution 7, 16, 23, 50

George III, King 35, 52
guinea (coin) 35, 61

Hargrave, Francis 57
Hawkins 3

Ibo tribe 29
Industrial Revolution 7, 31

Jamaica 24-25, 27-30, 32-33, 51
Jefferson, Thomas 52

Kerr, James 45-48

Lewis, T. 9, 12
Leclerc 51
liberalism 22, 23-24
Lisle, David 45, 47
Liverpool 4, 15
Long, Edward 29-32, 34
L'Ouverture 7, 26, 48-52

Manumission Acts (America)
52
Mansfield, Lord 12, 56-61
Middle Passage 4, 16, 59
Montserrat 41-42
mortality
slaves 4, 48-49
seamen 15

Nelson, Horatio 35, 40, 44
Nugent, Lady Margaret 24-28

Pitt, William 18, 23, 38
Print, The 16
Prosser, Gabriel 52-56
pseudo-science 32
public protest 20-21, 61

Quakers 42, 52, 61

racism 7, 29-32, 34-35
repatriation 7
Richmond (rebellion) 55-56
Royal Adventurers 35

Saint Domingue 48-52
seasoning 25
Seven Years War 40
Sharp, Granville 9-12, 16, 45,
48, 56
slave rebellion (America) 52-56
slaves, before the sugar boom 3
slaves, in sugar plantations 3-4,
26-27, 42, 47
slaves, shipping of 4, 14, 15, 16,
56, 59, 60
Somersett, James 12, 56-60
Southern States (American)
52-53
Steward, Charles 56
Strong, Jonathan 9, 44-48
sugar 3, 4, 25-27

Thicknesse, Phillip 32-35
triangular trade 4

value of slaves 4, 7, 59
Victoria, Queen 39
Virginia, rebellion 55-56

Washington, George 53
Wallace, William 58
Wedgwood, Josia 15, 20
West Indies 4, 7, 24-34, 41-44,
48-51
Wilberforce, William 16,
17-21, 26-27, 37